D1307161

Student Rights

Avery Elizabeth Hurt, *Book Editor*

GREENHAVEN

Published in 2018 by Greenhaven Publishing, LLC
353 3rd Avenue, Suite 255, New York, NY 10010

Library of Congress Cataloging-in-Publication Data

Names: Hurt, Avery Elizabeth, editor.
Title: Student rights / Avery Elizabeth Hurt, book editor.
Description: New York : Greenhaven Publishing, 2018. I Series: Issues that concern you
I Includes bibliographical references and index. I Audience: Grades 9-12.
Identifiers: LCCN 2017028507 I ISBN 9781534502253 (library bound) I 9781534502802
(paperback)
Subjects: LCSH: Students—Legal status, laws, etc.—United States—Juvenile literature.
I Students—Civil rights—United States—Juvenile literature. I Educational law and legislation—United States—Juvenile literature.
Classification: LCC KF4150 .S7775 2017 I DDC 344.73/0793--dc23
LC record available at https://lccn.loc.gov/2017028507

Manufactured in the United States of America

Website: http://greenhavenpublishing.com

CONTENTS

On December 20, 1787, Thomas Jefferson, who was then serving as minister to France, wrote to James Madison expressing his concerns with the recently drafted Constitution. The document was lacking something Jefferson believed to be crucial: a bill of rights, that is a specific declaration of the rights and protections guaranteed to the citizens of the new republic. A bill of rights, Jefferson wrote, "is what the people are entitled to against every government on earth, general or particular, & what no just government should refuse... ." The problem, as Jefferson saw it, was that the Constitution was perfectly clear on what the government could do, but contained very little mention of what the government could *not* do.

Jefferson was not the only person troubled that the Constitution did not contain a bill of rights; most ordinary citizens agreed, and the lack of a bill of rights seemed very likely to prevent ratification of the Constitution. Nonetheless the framers argued that it was not necessary to spell out specific rights because individual rights were implicit in the Constitution. In fact, Alexander Hamilton argued that specifically listing these protections might be a poor idea. Including a list of specific rights, he argued, might suggest that the government was permitted to do anything that was not expressly forbidden in the Constitution, and that listing freedom of speech, religion, the press, and so on, implied that these were the *only* rights the people had. (This problem was eventually addressed in the Ninth Amendment, which reads, "The enumeration in the Constitution, of certain rights, shall not be construed to deny or disparage others retained by the people.")

The debate was fierce, and the hard work and hard-won compromises that had been reached in drafting the original document were at risk. In the end, the states voted to ratify the Constitution only with the agreement that one of the first actions of the new government would be to draft a Bill of Rights. In the first Congress of the new nation, James Madison (the primary author of the Constitution) drafted a series of amendments to address these concerns. These first ten amendments to the Constitution were quickly ratified by the states and became the Bill of Rights of the United States of America.

And Americans have been defending those rights ever since.

Though the Bill of Rights is a fairly succinct and straightforward document, interpreting how those rights shall be applied and protected keeps an entire industry of lawyers and scholars busy. The situation can be especially murky when it comes to students. Though young Americans have many of the same rights adults do, there are some obvious limitations to those rights. Children cannot vote, purchase alcohol, or drive cars until they are of legal age, for example. However, in 1969, the US Supreme Court, in *Tinker v. Des Moines*, a case you will read more about in the coming pages, explicitly stated that young people do not surrender their rights when they enter the schoolhouse. However, the responsibilities of parents, teachers, and school administrators to keep the students in their charge safe and protect the rights of all students (and teachers and administrators as well) can sometimes cause them to limit (or attempt to limit) the freedoms and rights of those students. Students, their parents, and their attorneys have often had to step up and demand that student rights be protected.

For many years, students, schools, and the courts have tried to work out just how much freedom students have to refuse to participate in the Pledge of Allegiance or take part in devotionals. Courts have also, over the years, had to step in to enforce the constitutional principle of separation of church and state, which prevents public schools from taking any action to support religion of any kind. The right to freedom of religion, which was designed to protect an individual's right to worship as he or she chose without interference from the government, has been a particularly sticky point in schools over the years. What students can and cannot wear to school, what sorts of slogans or images they can have on T-shirts, and what they can post on their blogs have all been matters in which students have had to learn about and occasionally defend. Student journalists are currently working to get legislation passed in all fifty US states that would prevent school administrations from controlling and censoring the content of their publications—a right guaranteed to the professional press, but thanks to another Supreme Court decision, not a given for student journalists. Meanwhile, transgender students are engaged in a national battle to ensure their right to use the bathroom that corresponds to their gender identities rather than their gender at birth.

And what rights students have vary from state to state and can change from time to time. At the moment, in nineteen US states, it is legal for school officials to use corporal punishment as a disciplinary measure, thanks to a 1977 Supreme Court decision that ruled that "spanking" students did not violate their rights. Several organizations are working to get the practice banned in the states where it is still legal, but it is proving surprisingly difficult.

Even the right to read freely can be challenged in schools. Though students' rights to free speech has been throughly supported by the courts, schools can and do still remove books from school libraries and reading lists if members of the community object to the content of the books for pretty much any reason. Though it is unlikely that students will ever be given the "right" to read whatever they want or to demand that certain books be left on the shelves, the American Library Association regularly campaigns against this kind of censorship. The viewpoints in *Student Rights* (Issues That Concern You) explore these and other areas in which the issue of students' rights has come up both in the United States and in Canada, how people have dealt with the issue in different time and places, and how the courts have responded. Knowing your rights and how you can defend them is an essential responsibility.

ONE

Students in Public Schools Have Certain Rights

David L. Hudson Jr.

In the following excerpted viewpoint, constitutional scholar David L. Hudson Jr. details what rights public school students do and do not have. While, as minors, students most certainly do not give up their constitutional rights when they attend school, their rights are somewhat limited. The author explains the constitutional principles that limit student rights and the philosophy behind those principles. He then goes on to outline the major constitutional issues students are likely to encounter, including freedom of expression in speech, clothing, and writing; protection from censorship; and the right to not participate in the Pledge of Allegiance. Hudson is a First Amendment expert and adjunct professor of law at Vanderbilt University.

Public school students do not lose their constitutional rights when they walk through the schoolhouse doors. The U.S. Supreme Court has recognized that "students in school as well as out of school are 'persons' under our Constitution." This means that they possess First Amendment rights to express themselves in a variety of ways. They can write articles for the school newspaper, join clubs, distribute literature and petition school officials.

"K-12 Public School Student Expression Overview." by David L. Hudson Jr., Newseum Institute, www.newseum.org, September 28, 2002. Reprinted by permission of the First Amendment Center of the Newseum Institute.

In school, a student's constitutional rights are slightly more limited than they would be at home.

But public school students do not possess unlimited First Amendment rights. Two legal principles limit their rights. First, as the Supreme Court has said, minors do not possess the same level of constitutional rights as adults. Second, the government generally has greater power to dictate policy when it acts in certain capacities, such as educator, employer or jailer. For instance, a school principal can restrict a student from cursing a teacher in class or in the hallway. However, the principal would have limited, if any, authority to punish a student for criticizing a school official off-campus.

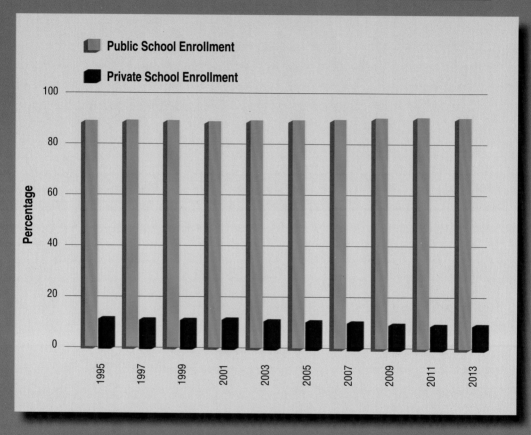

Percentage of US students enrolled in private elementary and secondary schools vs. public elementary and secondary schools, fall 1995 through fall 2013

Source: National Center for Education Statistics

This principle of greater government control applies broadly in the public schools. The paramount duty of public school officials is to educate children in a safe environment. As one federal court put it: "Learning is more important in the classroom than free speech."

However, public school officials act as arms of the government—state actors—and thus must respect the Bill of Rights and the First Amendment. The problem comes in ensuring that public school officials have authority to do their jobs without trampling on student free-expression rights. As Professor Erwin Chemerinsky said: "Schools cannot teach the importance of the First Amendment and simultaneously not follow it."

Balancing school officials' educational concerns against students' First Amendment rights is not easy. As the Supreme Court wrote: "Our problem lies in the area where students in the exercise of First Amendment rights collide with the rules of the school authorities."

These collisions seem to be occurring with increasing regularity, particularly in the wake of several high-profile school shootings culminating in the April 1999 tragedy at Columbine High School in Littleton, Colo. The post-Columbine period has seen a surge in the implementation of dress-code and zero-tolerance policies and a crackdown on student Internet speech.

Today, many First Amendment struggles occur in the public schools. Here are some of the leading issues:

Speaking Out in School

The First Amendment protects the right of citizens to express themselves in a variety of ways. Public school students, as young citizens, may engage in many modes of expression—from the words they speak to the ideas they write and even the clothes they wear.

Students can engage in political speech, which is considered the type of speech at the core of the First Amendment. The Founding Fathers considered such speech essential to the development of a constitutional democracy. The U.S. Supreme Court spelled out those rights in a case concerning public school students who spoke out on a major political issue of their time—the Vietnam War.

In the 1969 case *Tinker v. Des Moines Independent Community School District*, the high court ruled 7–2 that school officials violated the First Amendment rights of three Iowa students by suspending them for wearing black armbands to school. Even though the students were not technically speaking, the high court determined that the wearing of the armbands to protest the war was a form of symbolic speech "akin to pure speech." The court referred to the wearing of the armbands as a "nondisruptive, passive expression of a political viewpoint."

The Supreme Court established a protective standard for student expression in *Tinker*, which says that school officials cannot censor student expression unless they can reasonably forecast that the expression will cause a substantial disruption of school activities or will invade the rights others.

Though public school students possess the right to free speech, they are not free to express themselves in an unlimited form or fashion. In 1986, the Supreme Court ruled in *Bethel School District No. 403 v. Fraser* that school officials did not violate the First Amendment rights of a student suspended for giving a vulgar and lewd speech before the student assembly.

In *Fraser*, the high court wrote that "the freedom to advocate unpopular and controversial views in schools and classrooms must be balanced against society's countervailing interest in teaching students the boundaries of socially appropriate behavior."

In recent years, several students have been punished for writing poems, essays or displaying artwork that school officials deem disruptive or inappropriate. The school officials generally must show that they had a reasonable forecast (expectation that) the student expression would cause a substantial disruption. They cannot overreact with what the Supreme Court in *Tinker* called "undifferentiated fear or apprehension."

Some have argued that many schools have overreacted to a few sensational school shootings by clamping down on any student expression deemed offensive or disagreeable. Though school officials must ensure a safe learning environment, some fear that school officials have ignored students' First Amendment rights.

[...]

School Newspapers and Yearbooks

Many public school students who work on their school papers or yearbooks find that they do not have the freedom to write on certain controversial subjects. In 1988, the U.S. Supreme Court ruled in *Hazelwood School District v. Kuhlmeier* that public school officials can censor school-sponsored student expression as long as they have a valid educational reason for doing so.

This decision has given school officials broad authority to regulate school-sponsored publications. Generally, such publications are deemed to be non-public—as opposed to public—forums, which are defined as places that traditionally have been open to diverse viewpoints and First Amendment activity. A school can create a public forum when it "by policy or practice" opens up a publication for student control.

Several states have responded with so-called "anti-Hazelwood laws," which give greater free-expression protection to student journalists. Those states are Arkansas, Colorado, Iowa, Kansas, Massachusetts and Oregon. (California had adopted greater protection for student expression before the *Hazelwood* ruling.)

Underground Newspapers and Off-Campus Speech

Many students have turned to producing their own "underground" newspapers rather than writing for their school-sponsored papers. Students have more freedom to tackle controversial subjects in underground rather than school newspapers because the Supreme Court has afforded students more free-speech protection if the expression is student-initiated rather than sponsored by the school.

Students generally may distribute their underground newspapers at school as long as they do not create a substantial disruption of school activities. School officials, however, can enforce reasonable regulations with respect to the time, place and manner of distribution. School officials have even less authority to regulate off-campus speech—particularly if that expression is never distributed at the school.

But that doesn't mean school officials haven't tried. In fact, one Texas principal allegedly went so far as to try to prohibit a student from writing letters to the editor to the local town newspaper.

[...]

Cyberspeech

Many students have turned to the Internet to express a variety of viewpoints, including criticism of school officials. The U.S. Supreme Court has said that speech on the Internet is entitled to the highest level of protection on par with the print medium.

Students generally have broad freedom to express themselves on the Internet on their own time, using their own off-campus computers. However, some school officials have suspended students for their off-campus Internet postings that lampooned or criticized school officials or contained vulgar commentary.

Some courts have sided with the students, saying that school officials may not censor student speech unless they can reasonably forecast that the speech will cause a substantial disruption of the school environment or invade the rights of others. Other courts and commentators have said that school officials simply lack the authority to regulate students' off-campus behavior—on or off the Internet.

However, if a student creates certain online expression as part of a class or even using a school computer outside of class time, then school officials will argue that the speech is in fact school-sponsored and therefore subject to less protection.

Another major issue regarding cyberspeech concerns the use of filters. Federal and state laws require public schools and libraries to install filtering software to protect minors from harmful material on the Internet. At the federal level, the Children's Internet Protection Act requires public schools and libraries to install filtering software in order to receive federal monies for Internet hook-ups. Various states have passed laws that mandate the use of filters to screen out material that is harmful to minors.

Many free-expression advocates argue that filters block access to constitutionally protected materials. Many filters are imprecise and overbroad. The examples are numerous. For instance, sites mentioning the National Football League's Super Bowl XXXVI were blocked by a filter because they contain the term "XXX." Students and teachers also have complained that they have been denied access to online material that would help them in research projects and assignments.

Hate Speech and Speech Codes

Some school officials have implemented speech codes, arguing that they help to ensure a safe learning environment by prohibiting students from engaging in harassing speech or so-called hate speech. However, critics contend that some of the policies go too far and prohibit protected speech. A federal appeals court based in Pennsylvania struck down an anti-harassment policy for precisely that reason.

After the Columbine tragedy, it was reported that other, and particularly more popular, students ridiculed the two shooters. In response, some schools have targeted bullying. In 2001, Colorado passed a law requiring boards of education to adopt "a specific policy concerning bullying prevention and education." Other states have considered similar legislation. It remains to be seen whether these policies will be applied to speech that should be protected.

Sometimes it isn't students' speech but their choice of symbols that is interpreted by school officials as harassing or hateful. There is perhaps no symbol more controversial in the public schools than the Confederate flag, which supporters say is merely a symbol of heritage, but critics charge is a symbol of hate. Many students have been suspended for wearing such garb or even for drawing pictures of the flag in class.

Clubs

Students often form different clubs at school, including clubs that are not related to the school curriculum. In 1984, Congress passed the Equal Access Act, which forbids schools from discriminating against clubs, or denying them equal access to school facilities because of their philosophical or religious viewpoints. The act was largely passed to prevent widespread discrimination against religious clubs.

In 1990, the U.S. Supreme Court ruled in *Westside Community Board of Education v. Mergens* that the Equal Access Act was constitutional. In that case, the high court determined that a school district violated the Equal Access Act by denying use of its facilities to a religious club, while allowing a chess club, a scuba diving club and other "noncurriculum related" groups to use school facilities.

Under the law if a school opens its facilities to "any non-curriculum related group," it must open its facilities to all student groups. A recent area of controversy regarding student clubs involves the efforts of gay and lesbian students to obtain recognition for their groups.

TWO

Courts Have Affirmed the Rights of Students to Refuse to Pledge the Flag

Robert M. Schwartz, Esq. and Wayne Oppito, Esq.

> In the following viewpoint, Robert M. Schwartz and Wayne Oppito begin by using the example of a current controversy surrounding a professional athlete's refusal to stand for the US national anthem. They point out that there is no question that the ballplayer is legally exercising his right to free expression by refusing to stand or salute the flag. But does the same right apply to students in school? The authors transition their argument to the case of students, carefully laying out the case law and explaining to principals and teachers that students do indeed have the right to refuse to say the Pledge of Allegiance as long as the intent of their refusal is expression and not disruption. Robert M. Schwartz, Esquire, and Wayne Oppito, Esquire, are legal counsel for the New Jersey Principals and Supervisors Association.

In the last few weeks there has been much press coverage over San Francisco 49ers quarterback Colin Kaepernick's refusal to stand for the National Anthem. Some have criticized his action as being disrespectful to the men and women serving in the armed forces. Others, including President Obama, have pointed out that Kaepernick is merely exercising his constitutional right of free expression.

"Flag Salute – Rights of Students and Schools," by Robert M. Schwartz, Esq. and Wayne Oppito, Esq., New Jersey Principals & Supervisors Association, September 6, 2016. Reprinted by permission.

Are students obligated to pledge allegiance to the US flag?

That Kaepernick is exercising a constitutional right is not in dispute. As has been reported in the press, Kaepernick is not the first sports figure to use the Pledge of Allegiance or the National Anthem as a symbolic voice of protest. However unpopular Kaepernick's stance may be in certain quarters, the whole point of freedom of expression is to be able to express unpopular or controversial ideas.

What do you do if students decide to follow Kaepernick's example? Can students who choose to sit during the National Anthem or the Pledge of Allegiance be forced to stand at attention? The short answer is: no. Students, like Kaepernick, have the right to refuse to stand for the National Anthem or the Pledge of Allegiance, provided that they are exercising a mode of symbolic free expression and are not intending to be disruptive.

As the cases below demonstrate, the constitutional interpretations on this issue have evolved dramatically over the years.

In a 1937 case called *Hering, et al v. State Board of Education*, the Supreme Court of New Jersey addressed statutory language similar to N.J.S.A. 18A:36-3, except for the conscientious scruples exception. Two children, ages five and seven, were expelled from school because they refused to salute the flag and recite the Pledge of Allegiance. In challenging the expulsion, they claim that the statute was invalid because it infringed on the two students' religious freedom. The claim was rejected. The Court said:

> *Those who resort to educational institutions maintained with the State's money are subject to the commands of the State . . . . The performance of the command of the Statute in question could, in no sense, interfere with religious freedom. It is little enough to expect of those who seek the benefit of the education offered in the Public Schools of this State that they pledge allegiance to the Nation and the Nation's flag. The Pledge of Allegiance is, by no stretch of the imagination, a religious right. It is a patriotic ceremony which legislature has the power to require of those attending schools established at public expense. A child of school age is not required to attend the institutions maintained by the public. . . . Those who do not desire to conform with the commands of the statute can seek their schooling elsewhere.*
>
> *Hering v. State Board of Education, 117 N.J.L. 455, 456 (1937).*

As a result, the students' expulsion was affirmed.

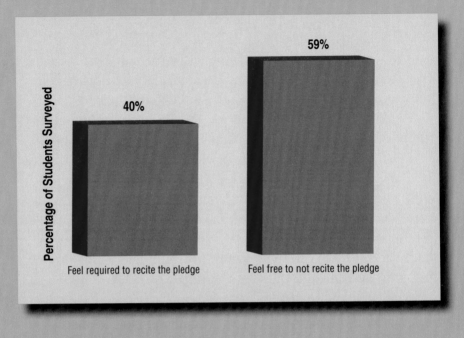

Perceived pressure to recite the Pledge of Allegiance among US students age thirteen through seventeen

40%

59%

Percentage of Students Surveyed

Feel required to recite the pledge

Feel free to not recite the pledge

Source: Gallup

In a 1942 decision, during World War II, the New Jersey Supreme Court appeared to back off the harsh result of the *Hering* case. In a matter entitled *In Re Latrecchia*, two children, ages and 13 and 14, who were Jehovah's Witnesses, were expelled from school because they would not salute the American flag. Subsequently, their parents were convicted of a disorderly persons offense because their children were not in regular attendance at school. The Court overturned the disorderly persons conviction of the children's parents because the children's failure to attend school was due to the school's decision to expel them—not because of anything that their parents did. With respect to the flag salute issue itself, while agreeing that the State was within its right to compel those who attend public schools to salute the flag, the Court quoting from another decision out of New York entitled

People v. Sandstrom said:

> *A salute of the flag is a gesture of love and respect ... fine when there is real love and respect. The flag is dishonored by a salute by a child in reluctant and terrified obedience to a command of secular authority which clashes with the dictates of conscience. The flag 'cherished by all our hearts' should not be soiled by the tears of a little child. The Constitution does not permit and the Legislature never intended, that the flag should be so soiled and dishonored.*

The Court concluded its decision by stating that "Liberty of conscience is not subject to uncontrolled administrative action."

In 1943, the United States Supreme Court weighed in on this issue in the matter of *West Virginia v. Barnette*. It ruled that a requirement that all pupils salute the flag was unconstitutional. The court said:

> *We think the action of the local authorities in compelling the flag salute and pledge transcends constitutional limitations on their power and invades the sphere of intellect and spirit, which it is the purpose of the First Amendment to our Constitution to reserve from all official control.* "The Court added, "If there is any fixed star in our constitutional constellation, it is that no official, high or petty, can prescribe what shall be orthodox in politics, nationalism, religion, or other matters of opinion or force citizens to confess by word or act their faith therein.*

This sentiment was fully adopted by the New Jersey courts in *Holden v. Board of Ed. of the City of Elizabeth*. The Petitioners there were a group of elementary-age students, suspended from school because they refused to salute the flag and repeat the Pledge of Allegiance. They claimed that, as Muslims, they were taught that it would be contrary to the teachings of Islam to pledge allegiance to any flag, whether the flag of Islam or the flag of the United States. For its part, the Board of Education of Elizabeth argued that the "exception for conscientious scruples was never intended to be so broadly construed as to include Petitioners' beliefs." The

Court found that the action of the Elizabeth Board of Education violated the children's constitutional rights. It held that:

> Neither our domestic tranquility in peace nor our martial effort in war depend on compelling little children to participate in a ceremony which ends in nothing for them but a fear of spiritual condemnation. If, as we think, their fears are groundless, time and reason are the proper antidotes for their errors. The ceremony, when enforced against conscientious objectors, more likely to defeat than to serve its high purpose, is a handy implement for disguised religious persecution. As such, it is inconsistent with our Constitution's plan and purpose.

The statute regarding flag salute is N.J.S.A. 18A:36-3. It states in relevant part that every board of education shall:

> Require the pupils in each school in the district on every school day to salute the United States flag and repeat the following pledge of allegiance to the flag: "I pledge allegiance to the flag of the United States of America and to the republic for which it stands, one nation, under God, indivisible, with liberty and justice for all," which salute and pledge of allegiance shall be rendered with the right hand over the heart, except that pupils who have conscientious scruples against such pledge or salute, or are children of accredited representatives of foreign governments to whom the United States government extends diplomatic immunity, shall not be required to render such salute and pledge but shall be required to show full respect to the flag while the pledge is being given merely by standing at attention, the boys removing the headdress.

In *Lipp v. Morris*, the Third Circuit of the United States Court of Appeals analyzed the scope of that statute's application. The plaintiff, a sixteen year old student, contended that the statutory requirement that she stand during the recitation of the Pledge of Allegiance violated her constitutional rights because it compelled her to make what she termed a "symbolic gesture." Relying on the U.S. Supreme Court decision in *West Virginia Board of Education v.*

Barnette, Lipp urged that her right to remain silent and not to be forced to stand during the Pledge of Allegiance was protected by the First Amendment. The Court agreed. The Court said that any requirement that she stand at respectful attention while the flag salute was being administered was an "unconstitutional requirement that the student engage in a form of speech" and therefore could not be enforced.

Based on this case law, as it stands today, students who refuse to stand for the Flag Salute or the National Anthem to make a political statement or act out of some discernible religious belief are exercising rights of free expression. This is not to mean that a teacher or an administrator can't ask students who refuse to stand, why they refuse. They can. And if a student who refuses to stand is under 18 years of age, the teacher or the administrator can discuss the matter with the student's parents, though administrators and teachers should be mindful that the constitutional right belongs to the student—not the parents. However, if the reasons given by the student amount to a form of symbolic political speech—protest over a government policy—or are based on religious beliefs and are not intended to be disruptive—the students' right of free expression may not be abridged.

THREE

Students Have the Right to Express Themselves Through Their Clothing

Anti-Defamation League

In the following viewpoint, the Anti-Defamation League offers guidelines and useful examples for when schools can and cannot enforce dress codes. Freedom of speech extends to freedom of expression, so that means it covers clothing as well as speech and writing. But when it comes to what students can and cannot wear to school, things can get complicated. As you shall see, enforceable dress codes are constitutional, but only within certain conditions and with exceptions—particularly for religious garments and symbols, such as yarmulkes, head scarves, and rosaries. The Anti-Defamation League is an international organization founded to protect the Jewish people and to secure justice and fair treatment for all people.

The First Amendment allows for mandatory uniform policies or dress codes in the public schools. However, it also generally permits exemptions from such policies or codes for students to wear religious clothes, head coverings, symbols or other attire. Under many circumstances policies or codes that prohibit students from wearing religious clothes or other attired are unconstitutional or unlawful.

"Dress Codes," by The Anti-Defamation League (www.adl.org). Reprinted by permission from The Anti-Defamation League.

The wearing of religious apparel in schools is generally permitted and supported but can be subject to the school's discretion.

Specific Issues and Questions

Under what circumstances are mandatory uniform policies or dress codes permissible under the First Amendment?

A student's decision about the clothes he or she wears is a form of expression.[1] Therefore, a limitation on clothing choices through uniform policies or dress codes must comply with the First Amendment's free speech clause.[2] What is required by the First Amendment depends on whether a policy or code is neutral to expression, or it differentiates among viewpoints or opinions.

Religious composition of younger millennials in the United States

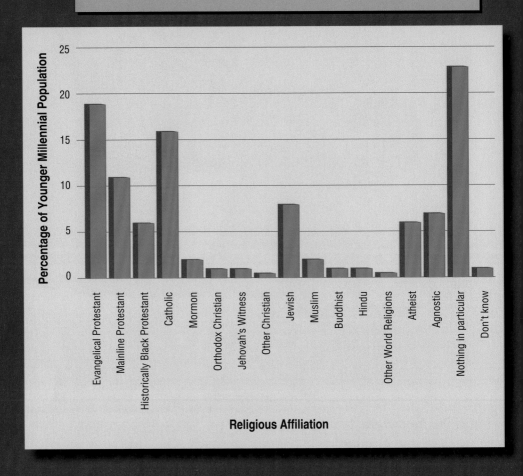

Source: Pew Research Foundation

Neutral Policies

Such policies as written and in application are not intended to suppress student expression or viewpoints.[3] To be valid under the First Amendment, neutral polices must meet three criteria. First, they must further an important or substantial government interest, which can include, increasing student achievement and focusing on learning, promoting safety, providing a more orderly school environment, encouraging professional dress, promoting school spirit, improving student self-esteem, or bridging socio-economic differences.[4] Second, the school interest in the code or policy must be unrelated to suppression of free expression. And third, any incidental restrictions on student expression must be no more necessary than to further or facilitate the government interest in the policy or code.[5] If other forms of student communications are available, including peer to peer communications, school newspapers, or school organizations, the third requirement is generally met.[6] Furthermore, policies or codes that allow students' clothes to bear small clothing logos, school logos or messages, or allow students to wear buttons bearing viewpoints do not generally transform them into policies or codes that differentiate among viewpoints or opinions.[7]

Policies Differentiating Among Viewpoints or Opinions

Such policies or codes censor or bar certain viewpoints or opinions, including religious viewpoints or expression.[8] They are valid under the following circumstances. First, where a school demonstrates that a particular message or expression causes a material or substantial disruption to the school environment, or school officials can reasonably forecast that the message will cause a material or substantial disruption.[9] Such a forecast cannot be based on mere speculation, but on prior events or history.[10] Second, the message is lewd, vulgar or sexual in nature.[11] Or third, the message promotes illegal drug use.[12]

Under What Circumstances Must Exemptions from a Uniform Policy or Dress Code Be Granted for Students to Wear Religious Clothes or Other Attire?

The public schools generally are permitted to accommodate the religious clothing and attire needs of students.[13] Provided that a uniform policy or dress code complies with the First Amendment's free speech clause and it is truly general in nature and neutral to religion, the policy or code may prohibit students from wearing religious clothes or attire so long as there is a nominal justification for the prohibition.[14] However, there are a number of significant exceptions to this rule. So under many circumstances schools will be required to exempt students from uniform policies or dress codes for the purpose of wearing religious attire.

State Laws

Approximately twenty states have laws—either by statute or court decision—called Religious Freedom Restoration Acts which require the government, including public schools, to demonstrate a narrow and compelling interest where religious activity or practice is substantially burdened by a law, ordinance, government rule or practice.[15] Demonstrating such an interest is extremely difficult. For the purposes of these laws, it is irrelevant whether or not the law, rule or practice is general in nature or neutral towards religion.

A uniform policy or dress code prohibiting a student from wearing religious clothes or attire will generally constitute a substantial burden on religious practice and will be impermissible under such state laws.

Uniform Policies or Dress Codes Targeting Religion

If a uniform policy or dress code is not neutral to religion and adversely treats religious activity or practice compared to secular activity, the First Amendment's free exercise clause requires that a school must demonstrate a narrow and compelling interest for the policy or code.[16] Under such circumstances, it is highly unlikely that the policy or code's prohibition on a student wearing religious clothes or attire will be constitutional.

There are several common circumstances where a policy or code is not neutral to religion. First, the language of the policy or code specifically targets religion or religious practice for adverse treatment.[17] Second, the policy or code may provide secular accommodations, for instance a medical exemption, but no similar exemption for religious practice.[18] Or third, the policy or code may be designed in a way that effectively targets religious, but not secular conduct.[19]

Uniform Policies or Dress Codes Raising Constitutional Issues in Addition to Free Exercise of Religion

Students, their parents or guardians sometimes bring other constitutional challenges to uniform polices or dress codes in addition to the free exercise of religion. Under such circumstances where there is another legitimate constitutional claim such as free speech or the right to direct a child's upbringing some courts will apply more rigorous scrutiny to a policy or code's prohibition on the wearing of religious clothes or attire.[20]

Some courts have required a demonstration of a narrow and compelling interest.[21] And other courts have required a lesser balancing test evaluating whether the policy or code places an undue burden on religious practice and whether the policy or code bears more than a reasonable relation to its stated objective.[22] Under either test, the policy or code will likely be unconstitutional.

The law in this area diverges by jurisdiction.[23] It is therefore highly advisable for school personnel, parents or guardians to consult with an attorney to determine the local standards.

Can schools ban the wearing of religious symbols in an effort to stop gang activity or violence?

Most courts evaluating prohibitions on gang activity in public schools that bar the wearing of religious symbols have found them unconstitutional on free speech or vagueness grounds.[24] Furthermore, the same exceptions to uniform policy and dress code bans on religious clothing would apply to prohibitions on gang activity that bar religious symbols. So if such a prohibition is issued in a state that has a Religious Freedom Restoration Act or if it is not neutral to religion, the ban would likely be unconstitutional. Additionally, if such a ban is challenged on free exercise of religion and other constitutional groups, it also may be subject to more rigorous scrutiny and be found unconstitutional. So in the aggregate, most bans on gang activity that bar the wearing of religious symbols will be unconstitutional or unlawful.

Sample Scenarios and Situations

Neutral Uniform Policy in State with a Religious Freedom Restoration Act

Zoe attends Farmdale Middle School. Zoe is Muslim and is required by her faith to wear a religious head covering called a Hijab. Over the summer the Farmdale School District adopts a viewpoint neutral mandatory dress code that prohibits the wearing of any hats or head coverings during the school day. Zoe's parents advise the Farmdale Middle School principal that their faith requires Zoe to wear a Hijab. They ask the principal for an accommodation to allow their daughter to wear the Hijab at school. Zoe lives in a state with a Religious Freedom Restoration Act.

Should the Principal Allow Zoe to Wear the Hijab to School?

The Farmdale School District has adopted a neutral mandatory uniform policy which complies with the First Amendment's free speech clause. Under the First Amendment, the principal could allow Zoe to wear the Hijab, so the question is whether he is required to do. Because Zoe lives in a state with a Religious Freedom Restoration Act, the school would have to demonstrate a narrow and compelling reason for why Zoe cannot wear the Hijab at school. It is highly unlikely that the school will be able to demonstrate such a reason. Therefore, the prohibition will be unlawful under the state Religious Freedom Restoration Act.

Neutral Dress Code that Allows Medical Exemptions

Jeff attends Western High School in Franklin County. Over Winter break, the Franklin County School District adopts a viewpoint neutral mandatory dress code that prohibits the wearing of hats or head coverings during the school day. However, the code allows medical exceptions, including to the head-covering prohibition. The policy also allows students to wear hats for head coverings for school-related activities such as sports and drama. Jeff's faith requires him to wear a Jewish head covering called a Yarmulke. On the first day back from break, Jeff wears his Yarmulke to school. His teacher tells him that under the new code he cannot wear his Yarmulke during the school day, tells Jeff to remove it, and advises Jeff that he could be suspended if he again wears the Yarmulke to school.

Can the School Bar Jeff From Wearing a Yarmulke to School?

Although the dress code is neutral for the purposes of free speech, it is not neutral towards religion for two reasons. First, it allows secular medical exceptions. And second, it allows students to wear hats or head coverings for school-sponsored student activities. Therefore, the school district will have to demonstrate a narrow and compelling interest for prohibiting Jeff from wearing a Yarmulke. It is highly unlikely that the district will be able to make this demonstration, and therefore the prohibition is unconstitutional under the First Amendment's free exercise clause.

Shirt Bearing a Religious Message

The Walton School District has a mandatory dress code requiring all students to wear collared blue, green or white shirts with khaki blue or tan pants or skirts. However, messages are permitted on shirts provided they are not disruptive, offensive, or do not promote illegal drug use. Sally, a high school student, wears to school a white collared shirt which states "Moses was the greatest prophet." Her teacher, Mr. Jones, believes that her shirt may offend other students and sends Sally to the school principal to make determination as to whether she can wear the shirt and remain at school for the day. The shirt has caused no disruption and there is no past history at the school of religious-related harassment or other incidents?

Can the Principal Prohibit Sally from Wearing the Shirt?

No. Although the shirt in question bears a religious message, the scenario raises a free speech issue. Under the dress code, Sally can wear a collared white shirt bearing a message. The shirt has caused no disruption, and furthermore there is no basis for school personnel to reasonably forecast a disruption. The shirt is not offensive as it is not lewd, vulgar or sexual in nature. And it does not promote illegal drug use. Therefore, Sally can wear the shirt to school.

Student Wearing Religious Symbol Is Suspended for Violating Gang Activity Policy

Robert, a middle school student, is Jewish. His grandfather recently gave him a silver Star of David necklace, which he wears to school. Very few Jewish children attend his school. David's school district has an anti-gang policy which prohibits students from wearing gang-affiliated colors, signs or symbols. The policy does not define the meaning of gang affiliated. Additionally, the school principal has full discretion to determine what colors, signs and symbols are gang related. The school principal sees David wearing the necklace and tells him that he cannot wear the necklace to school because the Star of David is a symbol used by certain gangs.

Can the Principal Prohibit David from Wearing His Necklace at School?

No. Although the anti-gang prohibition appears to be general and neutral towards religion, it is unconstitutionally vague for two reasons. First, it does not define the term "gang-related" and therefore provides no notice of what is and what is not a gang symbol. Second, the principal has full discretion to determine whether a symbol is gang-related and therefore any such determination is subjective.

Endnotes

[1] See Palmer v. Waxahachie Indep. School District, 579 F.3d 502 (5th Cir. 2009), cert denied, 130 S. Ct. 1055 (U.S. 2010); Jacobs v. Clark County School District, 526 F.3d 419 (9th Cir. 2008); Bar-Navon v. Brevard County School District, 290 Fed. Appx. 273 (11th Cir. 2008); Blau v. Fort Thomas Public School District, 401 F.3d 381 (6th Cir. 2005); Littlefield, et. al. v. Forney Indep. School District, 268 F.3d 275 (5th Cir. 2001); Canady v. Bossier Parish School Board, 240 F.3d 437 (5th Cir. 2001).

[2] Id.

[3] Id.

[4] Id.

[5] Id.

[6] Id.

[7] See Palmer, 579 F.3d 502; Jacobs, 526 F.3d 419; Littlefield, 268 F.3d 275; see also Frudden v. Pilling, 2015 U.S. Dist. LEXIS 16890 (D. Nev., Feb. 10,

2015) (elementary school had compelling interest in putting school motto on uniform).

8. See Nuxoll v. Indian Prairie School District, 636 F.3d 874 (7th Cir. 2011); B.W.A. v. Farmington R-& School District, 554 F.3d 734 (8th Cir. 2009); Barr v. Lafon, 538 F.3d 554 (6th Cir. 2008), rehearing, en banc, denied by, 553 F.3d 463 (2009), cert denied, 130 S. Ct. 63 (U.S.); Sapp v. School Board of Alachua County Florida, 2011 U.S. LEXIS 124943 (N.D. Fla. 2011); Nixon v. Northern Local School District Board of Education, et. al., 383 F. Supp. 2d 965 (S.D. Ohio 2005).

9. See Tinker v. Des Moines Indep. Community School District, 393 U.S. 503 (1969); Nuxoll, 636 F.3d 874 (T-shirt bearing the message "My Day of Silence, Straight Alliance" and "Be Happy, Not Gay" did not cause a material or substantial disruption); B.W.A., 554 F.3d 734 ; Barr, 538 F.3d 554 ; Sapp, 2011 U.S. LEXIS 124943 (T-shirt which stated in part "Islam is the Devil" caused a substantial disruption); Nixon, 383 F. Supp. 2d 965 (T-Shirt which said in part "Homosexuality is a sin, Islam is a lie, and Abortion is murder" did not cause a material or substantial disruption).

10. Id.

11. See Bethel School District v. Fraser, 478 U.S. 675 (1986); Nixon, 383 F. Supp. 2d 965 (T-shirt bearing the message "My Day of Silence, Straight Alliance" and "Be Happy, Not Gay" was not offensive within the meaning of Fraser).

12. See Morse v. Frederick, 551 U.S. 393 (2007).

13. See Employment Div. v. Smith, 494 U.S. 872, 890 (1990); see generally, Locke v. Davey, 540 U.S. 712 (2004).

14. See Smith, 494 U.S. 872.

15. The twenty states are Alabama, Alaska, Arizona, Connecticut, Florida, Idaho, Illinois, Indiana, Massachusetts, Minnesota, Missouri, New Mexico, Ohio, Oklahoma, Pennsylvania, Rhode Island, South Carolina, Texas, Washington, and Wisconsin.

16. See Church of the Lukumi Babalu Aye, Inc. v. City of Hialeah, 508 U.S. 520 (1993).

17. Id.

18. Id.

19. Id.

20. See Hicks v. Halifax County Board of Education, 93 F.Supp. 2d 649 (E.D. N.C. 1999); Chalifoux v. New Caney Indep. School District, 976 F.Supp. 659 (S.D. Tex. 1997).

21. See Chalifoux, 976 F. Supp. 659.

22. See Hicks, 93 F.Supp. 2d 649.

[23.] See Jacobs, 26 F.3d 419; Combs v. Homer-Center School District, 540 F.3d 231 (3rd Cir. 2008), cert denied, 555 U.S. 1138 (2009); Parker v. Hurley, 514 F.3d 87 (1st Cir. 2008), cert denied, 555 U.S. 815; Civil Liberties for Urban Believers v. City of Chicago, 342 F.3d 752 (7th Cir. 2003), cert denied, 541 U.S. 1096 (2004); Leebaert v. Harrington, 332 F.3d 134 (2nd Cir. 2003); Henderson v. Kennedy, 253 F.3d 12 (D.C. Cir. 2001), rehearing denied, 265 F.3d 1072, cert denied, 535 U.S. 986 (2002); Kissinger v. Board of Trustees of the Ohio State University, College of Veterinary Medicine, 5 F.3d 177 (6th Cir. 1993); Cornerstone Bible Church v. City if Hastings, 948 F.2d 464 (8th Cir. 1991); Society of Separationists v. Herman, 939 F.2d 1207 (5th Cir. 1991), aff'd, rehearing en banc, 946 F.2d 1373, aff'd on rehearing, 959 F.2d 1283 (1992), cert denied, 506 U.S. 866.

24. See Stephenson v. Davenport Community School District, 110 F.3d 1303 (8th Cir. 1997), rehearing, en banc, denied by, 1997 U.S. App. LEXIS 13019; Chalifoux, 976 F.Supp. 659 (S.D. Tex. 1997).

FOUR

Your T-Shirt Speaks, Too

First Amendment Center

In the following viewpoint, the authors at the First Amendment Center examine some recent cases in which students have gone to court to defend their right to express their social and political opinions via messaging on their shirts and other apparel. While the law on freedom of expression is clear, the details—especially when they involve speech that can be construed as hateful—can be murky. However, the authors point out, freedom can be messy, and that's one of the things that is wonderful about living in a free and diverse democratic society. The First Amendment Center is an organization that informs and educates the public about the First Amendment.

If you think students are apathetic these days, you haven't been reading their T-shirts.

From the Confederate flag to gay rights, student shirts are walking billboards for every conceivable cause—blaring messages that are often provocative, sometimes funny, but always difficult to ignore.

School officials are not amused. Eager to prevent controversy or conflict, many administrators overreact by banning all messages in the name of "safety, order and discipline."

But in the land of the free, it's hard to censor without a fight. Even kids who don't know much about the First Amendment or current law know a lot about "free speech." Heavy-handed school administrators often find themselves fighting a lawsuit.

"T-shirt rebellion in the land of the free," by Charles Haynes. First Amendment Center, Nashville, TN, Sunday, March 14, 2004. Reprinted by permission of the First Amendment Center of the Newseum Institute.

Is it constitutional for a public school system to ban clothing that celebrates the Confederate flag?

The Albemarle County, Va., school district probably didn't think twice when they passed a dress code policy that, among other things, prohibits students from wearing clothing that depicts images of weapons.

But when 13-year-old Alan Newsom was recently told to turn his National Rifle Association T-shirt inside out, he refused. Alan's lawsuit is working its way through the courts, but he won an important victory when a federal appeals court barred the school district from enforcing the policy while the lawsuit is pending. The court indicated that the dress code is too broad—and may be unconstitutional.

Sweeping attempts to shut down student speech frequently backfire. About a year ago, a Georgia school district decided to ban all T-shirts with the Confederate flag. Overnight the most popular

T-shirt was one that says: "Jesus and the Confederate Battle Flag: Banned From Our Schools But Forever in Our Hearts."

Meanwhile in North Carolina, a principal told students that he wouldn't allow "gay, fine by me" T-shirts in his school. A New Jersey school banned a T-shirt with the word "redneck." And so it goes around the nation.

School districts may win some of these lawsuits and fights—but they'll probably lose most of them. Here's why: In 1969, the U.S. Supreme Court ruled in *Tinker v. Des Moines Independent School District* that students don't "shed their constitutional rights to freedom of speech and expression at the schoolhouse gate."

The *Tinker* case involved several students who decided to wear black armbands to school to protest U.S. involvement in Vietnam. Hearing about the planned protest, school officials quickly enacted a no-armband policy. When the students were told they couldn't wear their armbands (even though other symbols were allowed), they sued.

In finding for the students, the Court made clear that school officials may not ban student expression just because they don't like it—or because they think it might cause conflict. The school must have evidence that the student expression would lead to either (a.) a substantial disruption of the school environment, or (b.) an invasion of the rights of others.

The *Tinker* standard gives strong protection to political and religious speech by students in public schools. And most courts are likely to view a wide range of student expression from "redneck" to "gay, fine by me" as protected speech—unless the school can demonstrate with reasonable evidence that the speech will cause a "substantial disruption."

Tinker isn't the last word, however. In a 1986 case (*Bethel v. Fraser*), the Supreme Court ruled that school officials could prohibit vulgar speech at a school assembly. Such speech, said the Court, is different from the purely political speech protected under *Tinker*. The Court put it this way:

> "[T]he freedom to advocate unpopular and controversial views in schools and classrooms must be balanced against

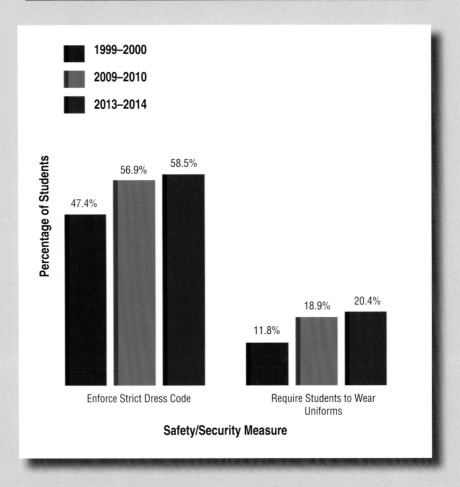

Percentage of US public schools that enforce a strict dress code and require students to wear uniforms, by school year

- 1999–2000
- 2009–2010
- 2013–2014

Percentage of Students

47.4%
56.9%
58.5%

Enforce Strict Dress Code

11.8%
18.9%
20.4%

Require Students to Wear Uniforms

Safety/Security Measure

Source: National Center for Education Statistics

society's countervailing interest in teaching students the boundaries of socially appropriate behavior."

Where does that leave school officials? The courts have given them a free hand to ban student speech that is clearly vulgar, lewd or obscene. And the courts mostly defer to administrators to regulate student speech that is "school-sponsored" (as in the school newspaper). But all other student speech is still protected under *Tinker.*

Consider the case of Elliot Chambers, the Minnesota student who was told that he couldn't wear a shirt with the message "Straight Pride." The school claimed that the shirt offended some students and pointed out that there had been several hostile incidents involving gay students.

But Chambers sued, saying that the ban on his shirt was unconstitutional. A federal district court agreed. Applying *Tinker,* the judge found that Chamber's shirt was not directly connected to the disruptions claimed by the school.

"While the sentiment behind the 'Straight Pride' message appears to be one of intolerance," wrote the judge, "the responsibility remains with the school and its community to maintain an environment open to diversity and to educate and support its students as they confront ideas different from their own."

Is ensuring "an environment open to diversity" sometimes messy or offensive? Of course it is. That's what freedom is all about. Most Americans wouldn't have it any other way.

FIVE

Student Bloggers Have Rights—and Limitations

Electronic Frontier Foundation

> In the following viewpoint, an excerpted FAQ on student blogging, students get answers to their most commonly asked questions about the rights and responsibilities concerning both their school and personal blogs. Not too many years ago, official school newspapers and other such publications were the primary way that students could make their opinions known to a large audience. Blogging changed that almost overnight. Student bloggers enjoy more rights than you may think, but a careful reading of this viewpoint shows that there are limitations to those rights as well. The Electronic Frontier Foundation is a nonprofit organization that defends civil liberties in the digital world.

Can Public High School Administrators Censor What I Say in a School-Hosted Blog or Other School-Sponsored Publication?

Usually, but it depends on the facts. In *Hazelwood Sch. Dist. v. Kuhlmeier*, 484 U.S. 260 (1988), the Supreme Court distinguished a school-sponsored newspaper from the armbands permitted in *Tinker* and allowed censorship that was "reasonably related to legitimate pedagogical concerns." This rule is referred to as the *Hazelwood* standard or the *Hazelwood* test. The *Hazelwood* standard applies to censorship of "school-sponsored publications, theatrical productions, and other expressive activities that students,

Blogging can be a great way to express yourself, but make sure you know which rights you do—and don't—enjoy as a student blogger.

parents, and members of the public might reasonably perceive to bear the imprimatur of the school." "Imprimatur of the school" refers to activities that appear to be sponsored or endorsed by the school.

The *Hazelwood* standard is less protective of your rights than the *Tinker* test. However, there is one bright spot: the *Hazelwood* standard does not apply to publications that have been opened as "public forums for student expression," even if those publications are school-sponsored.

[...]

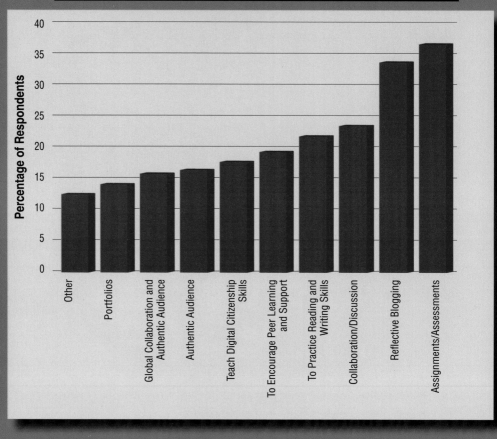

Why student blogs are being used, according to educator respondents

Percentage of Respondents

- Other
- Portfolios
- Global Collaboration and Authentic Audience
- Authentic Audience
- Teach Digital Citizenship Skills
- To Encourage Peer Learning and Support
- To Practice Reading and Writing Skills
- Collaboration/Discussion
- Reflective Blogging
- Assignments/Assessments

Source: The Edublogger

Do I Have More Protections for a Personal Blog?

Yes. In *Emmett v. Kent School District*, 92 F. Supp.2d 1088 (W.D. Wash. 2000), the court held that public school officials had violated a student's First Amendment rights by punishing the student for his personal website, the "Unofficial Kentlake High Home Page." The court held that "although the intended audience was undoubtedly connected to Kentlake High School, the speech was entirely outside of the school's supervision or control." Likewise, in *Flaherty v. Keystone Oaks School Dist.*, 247 F.Supp.2d 698 (W.D. Pa. 2003) a federal court found a public school's policy, which prohibited "inappropriate, harassing, offensive or abusive" behavior, was unconstitutional because "the policy could be (and is) read by school officials to cover speech that occurs off school premises and that is not related to any school activity in an arbitrary manner."

Sweet, My Personal Blog Is Untouchable!

Not so fast. EFF believes that public schools have no right to punish or censor any speech activities conducted outside of the school gates, and the Supreme Court has yet to consider such off-campus censorship. However, some lower courts have applied the *Tinker* "material disruption" standard in cases concerning the personal web sites of high school and middle school students. For example, in *Beussink v. Woodland School District*, 30 F. Supp.2d 1175 (E.D. Mo. 1998), a federal court applied *Tinker*'s "material disruption" standard when considering a student's web site that used vulgar language to criticize his public school and its teachers and administrators. Even though the site was created on the student's own time, with his own computer and Internet connection, the court decided that the *Tinker* "material disruption" test applied since a classmate viewed the site at school. While it is unfortunate that the court applied the less protective standard, in the end the student was vindicated—since there was no material disruption, the court decided that the student's First Amendment rights were violated.

[...]

So Can I Criticize Teachers on My Blog?

It depends on how you do it. Merely criticizing or insulting schoolteachers and administrators, even with vulgar language, likely will not amount to the "material disruption" required by the Supreme Court. See e.g. *Beidler v. North Thurston County (Wash.) Sch. Dist.*, No. 99-2-00236-6 (Thurston Cty. Super. Ct. July 18, 2000) (unpublished opinion holding the First Amendment protected a student's private web site that ridiculed a school administrator), and *Beussink v. Woodland School District*, 30 F. Supp.2d 1175 (E.D. Mo. 1998) (student's vulgar criticisms of school on his personal blog did not rise to a "material disruption.").

However, if you publish anything that might be considered a physical threat toward a student, teacher, or administrator, a court will likely find that punishment by the school is constitutional. See *J.S. ex rel H.S. v. Bethlehem Area School District*, 569 A.2d 638 (Pa. 2002) (punishment of student for publishing an image of decapitated teacher and soliciting donations for a hit man on his personal blog was justified under the "material disruption" test, even though it was intended as a joke and a law enforcement investigation concluded the student was not a threat).

Similarly, although your opinions are protected by the First Amendment, publishing defamatory content—even jokingly—may get you in trouble at school, and maybe even get you sued. Other types of speech may also violate the law and put you within reach of the school's discipline, so read further to see what legal pitfalls you should avoid.

Can I Publish Sexual Content on My Blog?

Yes, as long as it's not obscene. However, it's important to note that obscenity law applies differently to minors and adults. In *Ginsberg v. New York*, 390 U.S. 629, the Supreme Court found a lower standard of obscenity applies when the speech is directed toward minors: speech is obscene as to minors (or "harmful to minors") if it (1) appeals to the prurient, shameful, or morbid interest of minors, (2) is patently offensive to prevailing standards in the adult community as a whole with respect to what is suitable for minors, and (3) is utterly without redeeming social importance for minors.

To steer clear of this law, avoid posting images that most people in your community would consider to be pornographic, especially "hard-core" porn that depicts actual sexual acts. However, you do have a clear constitutional right to post explicit sexual content that isn't just meant to be arousing, but is related to social issues like sexual health that are important to minors.

What Can I Do to Avoid Causing a "Material Disruption" at School with My Personal Blog?

Based on how the courts have applied the "material disruption" standard to off-campus web sites in the past, there are several things you can do to avoid a situation where the school might discipline you:

- Most importantly, don't post anything that someone at school is likely to take as a direct physical threat against school staff or students.

- Don't advocate for the immediate violation of any laws or school rules.

- Review the Bloggers' Legal Guide to understand your rights and make sure you aren't publishing anything illegal. Just as you have First Amendment rights like other bloggers, you're also subject to all the same legal responsibilities.

- Don't use any school resources to publish or view your blog.

- Don't encourage other students to read or post comments to your blog while at school—tell them to wait until they are off campus. If you see comments on your blog posted by other students during school hours, consider deleting them.

- Make sure it's clear to readers that the blog isn't sponsored by or affiliated with the school.

- Before you start cussing or bagging on people, take a second to cool off. Although we think you have a right to use coarse language to describe people at school, and several courts have agreed with us, it will still increase the chance that your school will try to punish you.

What if I Want to Advocate Civil Disobedience on my Blog?

If you want to, for example, call for a student walk-out or otherwise advocate for civil disobedience that might be considered a "material disruption" at school, or if you just want to be able to freely criticize teachers and students without fear of getting unjustly punished, you should blog anonymously.

Even if you're blogging anonymously, though, you still shouldn't publish anything illegal—first off, you don't want to break the law, and second, publishing illegal material will increase the chance that someone will try to subpoena your Internet Service Provider or your blog host for your real identity. If you are notified that someone is trying to subpoena your real identity and you don't have a lawyer, contact EFF—we may be able to help.

[…]

What if I Get Punished for My Personal Blog?

Contact your lawyer; if you don't have one, contact EFF and we may be able to help. Even those courts that have used the "material disruption" test when evaluating school punishments for off-campus web sites have usually found the punishments to be unconstitutional. In fact, some students who have been punished for their personal web sites have been able to get their school records cleared and obtain cash settlements from their schools in exchange for dropping or not bringing a lawsuit. For example, Oceanport School District school administrators in New Jersey punished an eighth grader for his website that was critical of the school, and ended up having to pay him $117,500 to settle his First Amendment lawsuit.

Most schools, when faced with the threat of a suit for a clearly unconstitutional punishment, will back down and clear your record.

[…]

Should I Blog About My Fellow Students' Private Lives?

Not without asking. People can get upset if you spread their secrets. Ask friends and family what types of stuff they're comfortable with you sharing on your blog. When you take pictures for your online photo album, be considerate and ask your subjects if they don't mind before you post it.

[…]

What About Blogging About My Own Private Life?

Keep in mind that whatever you post on a public blog can be seen by your friends, your enemies, your teachers, your parents, your ex, that Great Aunt who likes to pinch your cheeks like you're a baby, the admissions offices of schools and colleges to which you might apply, current and future potential employers, and anyone else with access to the Internet and a search engine. While you can change your blog post at any time, it may be archived by others.

So, before you reveal personal information online, carefully consider whether you want that to be public now and in the future. And keep in mind that although a school has little power to punish you for off-campus speech, it can still use your blog against you as evidence of other rules violations. For example, several underage college students were recently punished for violating their school's alcohol policy after they posted pictures of themselves drinking.

What Can I Do to Blog More Privately?

You can use password-protected blogs and other technologies that allow a more limited audience, such as "friends-only" posts. If you don't want to blog anonymously, consider blogging under only your first name, or for even more privacy, a pseudonym. This will make it harder for people to search on your name (depending, of course, on how rare your name is). You can also use a robots .txt file to stop search engines from indexing blog pages you don't want crawled.

SIX

Student Journalists Deserve Legislative Protections

Roxann Elliott

> In the following viewpoint, Roxann Elliot reports on how New Voices legislation is being drafted in Indiana and what the new laws do and do not mean for the rights of student journalists. New Voices legislation, which as of this writing had been passed in ten states, is a countermeasure to a 1988 Supreme Court decision, *Hazelwood v. Kuhlmeier*. The legislation protects student journalists from administrative censorship and gives them many of the same rights and protections that professional journalists enjoy. At the time this article was written, Elliott was a publications fellow of the Student Press Law Center (SPLC).

The New Voices campaign is sprinting off the block this year with the first anti-*Hazelwood* legislation of 2017 being filed in Indiana.

Representative Ed Clere, R-New Albany, introduced House Bill 1130 Tuesday, kicking off the second attempt in Indiana's history to enact legal protections for high school and college journalists in the Hoosier State.

"I expect there will be a lot of support and I'm also anticipating a certain level of resistance," Clere told the SPLC, noting it was too early in the process to gauge support for the bill within the general assembly.

"New Voices legislation launched in Indiana," by Roxann Elliott, Student Press Law Center–SPLC, January 6, 2017. Reprinted by permission.

Student journalists are unprotected in the majority of US states.

That said, Clere and other proponents of the bill are putting together a comprehensive case and drawing on grassroots support.

Diana Hadley serves as the executive director of the High School Press Association, and she says Clere's involvement was a welcome surprise.

"He volunteered to sponsor this bill," Hadley said. "We had a grassroots campaign going, but we didn't have sponsors, yet. We were talking about who the sponsors might be and going over the possibilities and all of a sudden I get a call from Jim Lang at Floyd Central [High School] and he said Ed Clere is willing to sponsor a New Voices bill."

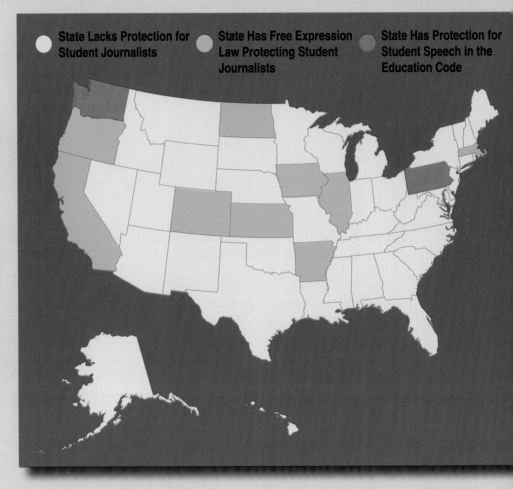

State Lacks Protection for Student Journalists

State Has Free Expression Law Protecting Student Journalists

State Has Protection for Student Speech in the Education Code

Source: Indiana Daily Student

Hadley was involved in another attempt to pass similar legislation in the late 1990s. She pointed out that the previous bill passed the state House, but failed in the Senate after opposition arose from associations representing Indiana principals, school boards and superintendents.

Clere, she said, understood the need to bring everyone together, and that's exactly what he's done.

"We get together with him and he says, 'Now, I want this to be educational. And my idea is that we choose five high school and five college student journalists to help draft the bill.'"

After an application process, Clere and Hadley enlisted five high school students and five college students from around the state to help research and draft the bill with insight gathered from similar laws in other states.

The group gathered on Dec. 7 to meet with representatives of several professional administrative and teaching associations to discuss the bill and present their case.

The bill, as written, includes protections for high school and college journalists to research and report the news in their schools, as decided by their own editorial staff, without interference by their administrations.

It also provides a safeguard for journalism advisers against administrative retaliation for supporting their students' right to report freely.

Clere is quick to assure parents and teachers that this law does not establish a carte blanche policy for students to print or broadcast whatever they please. In addition to restrictions on libel and invasion of privacy, the bill specifies that student content cannot "materially and substantially disrupt the operation of the public school."

"It's not a blanket license to say whatever you want," Clere said. "It simply gives student journalists the same right to express themselves that other journalists have and, importantly, it also holds them to the same standards in the same way a working journalist can't get away with libel or invasion of privacy or any other kind of unlawful act."

For Clere, the protections offered with the New Voices bill hit close to home.

"It's an issue I've been interested in ever since I was a high school journalist," Clere said, saying that he started his freshman year in the fall of 1988, immediately after the *Hazelwood v. Kuhlmeier* decision was handed down.

"I became aware of the New Voices movement and contacted a few folks including the journalism teacher at my old high school who is now my 15-year-old daughter's journalism teacher," Clere said.

"I'm interested in this for the benefit of all student journalists including my own daughter."

Hadley, likewise, has longstanding experience with scholastic journalism and the fallout from the *Hazelwood* decision. She advised the student newspaper at Mooresville High School for 33 years, later working on the yearbook and starting a broadcast news course.

She pointed out that *Hazelwood* wasn't, strictly speaking, the death-knell for student journalism. In her experience, supportive schools remained supportive, but restrictive schools got worse.

"I think that at schools where there had been some adversity —that administrators took it as the opportunity to clamp down."

In her own case, the principal at Mooresville maintained an open dialogue with herself and the student journalists.

"He met me at the desk, that morning, afterwards, and he said, 'Well, when do I show up for paste-up?'" Hadley recalls, referencing the term used in the industry for putting the paper together for print.

"I wasn't expecting that, and I said 'Well, Tuesday night, are you going to be there?' And he just grinned and said, 'Nah, you be sure to tell your kids it's business as usual at Mooresville High School.'"

Hadley was fortunate, and her principal went on to win "administrator of the year" awards from the National High School Press Association. But the New Voices campaign seeks to guarantee that the quality of scholastic journalism and student expression isn't susceptible to the vagaries of administrative turnover.

More importantly, Clere points out, the bill fosters responsibility. Young adults in Indiana can vote in their primaries at 17, provided they'll turn 18 before the general election.

"There are many students who can vote but they could be censored for writing or producing other content why they voted the way they did."

The bill has been assigned to the House Committee on Education.

Ten states now have statutes protecting the ability of student journalists at public institutions to choose the content of student media, with the addition of Illinois and Maryland in 2016. The campaign to enact curative legislation nationwide is known as New Voices after the John Wall New Voices Act that became law in North Dakota in 2015.

SEVEN

Free Speech on Campus Is in Trouble

Greg Lukianoff

In the following excerpted viewpoint, Greg Lukianoff argues that colleges and universities have long been banning and otherwise interfering with students' free speech rights, often unfairly blaming the Office of Civil Rights for these restrictions. Universities often misinterpret federal restrictions on harassment as a directive to limit free speech in order to protect their federal funding. More disturbing, the author argues, is the tendency of students to protect themselves from free speech by refusing to allow people with unpopular opinions to speak on campus. Lukianoff is an attorney and the president and CEO of the Foundation for Individual Rights in Education (FIRE).

2015 will be remembered as a year in which campus free speech issues took center stage, receiving extensive coverage in outlets like the *New York Times*, *Wall Street Journal*, *The Atlantic*, *Slate*, *Vox*, and *Salon*. Even President Obama voiced concerns about the lack of debate on college campuses.

For those of us who have been fighting campus censors for years, it's hard not to ask: "Where has everyone been?"

My organization, the Foundation for Individual Rights in Education (FIRE), has been defending freedom of expression on campus since 1999. We can attest that free speech, open inquiry, and academic freedom have *always* been threatened on campus by one force or another, even long before we were founded.

"Campus Free Speech Has Been in Trouble for a Long Time," by Greg Lukianoff, The Cato Institute, January 4, 2016. Reprinted by permission.

Many believe that college students are standing in the way of free speech on their own campuses.

[...]

What Has Changed: Students Using Their Free Speech to Limit Free Speech

The biggest and most noticeable change in campus censorship in recent years has been the shift in student attitudes. Today, students often demand freedom *from* speech rather than freedom of speech.

Media coverage of the campus free speech crisis exploded in 2014 after a rash of "disinvitations"—student and faculty attempts to disinvite controversial speakers from campus, including former Secretary of State Condoleezza Rice and International Monetary Fund head Christine Lagarde.

Attention from the media has increased as more student-led efforts have gained popularity, such as demands for "trigger warnings" and "safe spaces," and efforts to police so-called "microaggressions." Critiquing PC culture is nothing new for conservative outlets, but even left-leaning authors at the *New Republic, The*

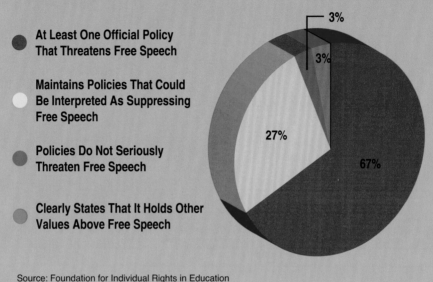

Private and Public US Colleges and Universities Rated by Speech Codes

- At Least One Official Policy That Threatens Free Speech
- Maintains Policies That Could Be Interpreted As Suppressing Free Speech
- Policies Do Not Seriously Threaten Free Speech
- Clearly States That It Holds Other Values Above Free Speech

3%

3%

27%

67%

Source: Foundation for Individual Rights in Education

Nation, New York Magazine, and the *New York Times* have been writing extensively about how these trends reflect very new, often alarming student attitudes about open discourse.

In my 15 years at FIRE, students have historically been *the most reliably pro-free-speech constituency on campus.* Students often showed more common sense than the professoriate, and certainly much more than the administrators.

But when stories about campus race-related protests inundated the news in the fall of 2015, I knew something had changed. It began when students at Wesleyan University demanded that the school's primary student newspaper be defunded after it published a student op-ed that was critical of the Black Lives Matter movement. Shortly after, Wesleyan's student government unanimously approved a resolution that will tentatively cut the paper's printing budget by half.

Things escalated when I saw firsthand that Yale students were demanding the resignations of two faculty members for sending out an email that questioned whether universities should tell students what they should or shouldn't wear as Halloween costumes.

Then, just days later, student protests at the University of Missouri soured when protesters manhandled a student journalist.

These protests put First Amendment defenders and free speech advocates like me in a somewhat difficult position. Of course, I'm supportive of students exercising their free speech rights. Indeed, I find it refreshing that students have overcome their oft-diagnosed apathy towards serious social issues. However, it's distressing that many of the protesters are using their free speech to demand limitations on others' free speech. The irony of these demands was particularly prominent at the University of Missouri, where FIRE recently helped pass a state law making it illegal to limit free speech activities on public university campuses to tiny zones. This new law helped make the Mizzou students' protests possible. But in a twist, the protesters created *their own* free speech exclusion zone to prevent media from covering the protest.

Now student protesters at at least 75 American colleges and universities have released lists of demands "to end systemic and structural racism on campus." Although this is a laudable goal, a troubling number of these demands would prohibit or chill campus speech.

For example, many of the demands try to make the expression of racial bias, which is generally protected speech, a punishable offense. At Johns Hopkins University, protesters demand "impactful repercussions" for anyone who makes "Black students uncomfortable or unsafe for racial reasons." Similarly, protesters at Georgia's Kennesaw State University demand "strong repercussions and sanctions" for those who commit "racist actions and racial bias on campus." And Emory University protesters want a bias response reporting system and sanctions for even "unintentional" acts or behaviors, including "gestures."

Others go as far as to mandate that universities forbid "hate speech." At Missouri State University, protesters demand that administrators announce a "commitment to differentiating 'hate speech' from 'freedom of speech.'" Protesters at Dartmouth College want "a policy with serious consequences against hate speech/ crimes (e.g. Greek house expelled for racist parties)." Similarly, student protesters at the University of Wyoming demand that the code of conduct be revised to hold students accountable for hate speech, complete with "a detailed reporting structure."

The evidence that today's students value freedom of speech less than their elders is not just anecdotal. In October, Yale University's William F. Buckley, Jr. Program released a survey that found that 51 percent of U.S. college students favor campus speech codes, and that 72 percent support disciplinary action against "any student or faculty member on campus who uses language that is considered racist, sexist, homophobic or otherwise offensive." These troubling results were echoed by a November 2015 global survey from Pew Research Center finding that a whopping 40 percent of U.S. millennials [ages 18–34] believe the government should be able to punish speech offensive to minority groups (as compared to only 12 percent of the Silent generation [70–87 year-olds], 24 percent of the Boomer generation [51–69 year-olds], and 27 percent of Gen Xers [35–50 year-olds]).

Conclusion

Thankfully, through old strategies and new ones, we can improve the climate for free speech on campus. Just one student or professor can protect free expression for thousands, or even hundreds of thousands, by filing a lawsuit against his or her school with the help of FIRE's Stand Up For Speech Litigation Project. SUFS is undefeated so far and has resulted in seven settlements that send the clear message to institutions that it will be expensive to ignore their obligations under the First Amendment. What's more, with every speech-protective judgment, it becomes harder for administrators to defend themselves with "qualified immunity," which shields individuals from personal liability where the law isn't clear.

[...]

How do we teach a generation about the value of free expression when speech is too often presented as a problem to be overcome, rather than part of the solution to many social ills? This is our great challenge, and it must be faced with both determination and creativity if the always-fragile right of freedom of speech is to endure.

Students Have a Right to Protection from Bodily Searches

Amy E. Feldman

> The intersection of freedoms and protections is often a delicate spot for protection of constitutional rights, sometimes especially so in schools, where teachers and administrators are responsible for the safety as well as the education of their students. In the following viewpoint, Amy E. Feldman examines a case in a Canadian school in which students were strip-searched by a math teacher. The author examines similar previous cases in the United States and determines that this search would have been unconstitutional if done in the United States. Feldman is the legal education consultant to the National Constitution Center.

A high school in Quebec recently came under fire after 28 students who were taking a math test were strip-searched by teachers. The teacher had asked the students to place their cellphones on her desk during the exam, and when one cell phone went missing, all of the students were called into a room, told to strip, and then searched to see who had taken the phone.

In the United States, that would have been a good test in constitutionality—and one that the teachers would have failed. What rights does a public school have to search its students? It had some rights, but not unlimited rights.

"When does a public school have the right to search its students?" by Amy E. Feldman, Constitution Daily– National Constitution Centre, May 31, 2013. Reprinted by permission.

The Fourth Amendment protects students from search and seizure. But there are notable exceptions when it does not.

The question of when a public school can search a student or a student's locker, backpack, purse, or other possessions first came before the Supreme Court in 1985.

A few girls at a high school girl in Piscataway, New Jersey, were caught smoking in the bathroom. After they were brought to the principal's office, the principal searched through the purse of one of the girls, known in court documents as T.L.O. (the initials were used to protect her privacy as a minor), and found cigarettes and evidence of drug dealing.

The student was suspended and received a year of probation. She sued the school district, claiming that it didn't have a warrant to search for contraband and therefore had conducted an unreasonable search.

The Supreme Court, in considering *New Jersey v. T. L. O.*, looked to the Fourth Amendment, which states, "The right of the people to be secure in their persons, houses, papers, and effects, against unreasonable searches and seizures, shall not be violated, and no Warrants shall issue, but upon probable cause, supported by Oath or affirmation, and particularly describing the place to be searched, and the persons or things to be seized."

Justice Byron White, who wrote the decision of the Supreme Court, said that the Fourth Amendment not only prevents the police from conducting unreasonable searches and seizures, but that "equally indisputable is the proposition that the 14th Amendment protects the rights of students against encroachment by public school officials."

Justice White stated that "the legality of a search of a student should depend simply on the reasonableness, under all the circumstances, of the search." The court stated that in order to be reasonable, the search could not be excessively intrusive.

Given that the search of the purse was not, according to the court, unreasonable or excessively intrusive, T.L.O. lost her case. That said, the case provides the requirement for schools and the protection for students that schools must show that a search of a student is reasonable given the circumstances.

T.L.O.'s case was at the heart of the case brought by then-13- year-old Savana Redding, who was strip-searched down to her underwear by officials at her middle school who suspected that she was hiding over-the-counter ibuprofen tablets.

Savana sued her school district, claiming unreasonable search and seizure, and her case went all the way to the Supreme Court.

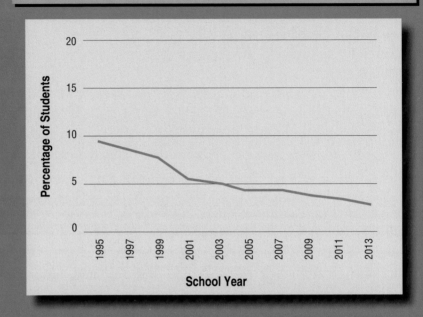

Percentage of US students ages twelve to eighteen who reported criminal victimization of theft or violent victimization at school

Percentage of Students

20

15

10

5

0

1995 1997 1999 2001 2003 2005 2007 2009 2011 2013

School Year

Source: National Center for Education Statistics

In the case of *Safford Unified School District v. Redding*—25 years after the T.L.O. case—the Supreme Court found that Savana's rights had, in fact, been violated and stated that a search by a school must not be "excessively intrusive in light of the age and sex of the student and the nature of the infraction."

Given that 13-year-old Savana was accused of having an over-the-counter medication, forcing her to strip was excessively intrusive and therefore unreasonable.

In an age in which school shootings are an unfortunate occurrence and drugs on high school grounds are common, no court has said that schools are prohibited from searching students—even strip-searching students—particularly in cases that involve the suspicion of weapons or contraband on the school grounds.

If you look at your district's policy, it will likely contain an explanation of when and how it will conduct searches.

As for the Canadian high school that conducted a strip-search after a math exam to find a cell phone, the facts simply don't add up under American constitutional law to find that such a search would be considered reasonable.

NINE

Many States Still Allow Corporal Punishment in Schools

Tim Walker

> You might think it is a given that students have the right to protection from physical assault by their teachers or other school officials, but, believe it or not, that is not necessarily the case, at least in nineteen US states. In the following viewpoint, Tim Walker examines the data on corporal punishment in US schools and notes that the practice is more often used in southern (and some western) states and more often against black males and children with disabilities. He also shares the opinions of experts who have shown that the practice has not proven effective and can be very damaging to students. Walker is a contributor to *NEA Today*, a publication of the National Education Association.

In 1977, the U.S. Supreme Court legitimized the use of corporal punishment in schools by deciding that the practice did not qualify as "cruel and unusual punishment." Despite the ruling in *Ingraham v. Wright*, corporal punishment—the use of physical force (usually paddling) on a student intended to correct misbehavior—would soon decline rapidly across the country. Between 1974 and 1994, 25 states would ban the practice, recognizing that it was an ineffective and inappropriate school discipline measure.

"Why Are 19 States Still Allowing Corporal Punishment in Schools?" by Tim Walker, National Education Association, October 17, 2016. Reprinted by permission.

Although paddling has fallen out of favor, corporal punishment is still used in many US schools.

Since the mid-1990s, however, only five more states have joined those ranks, leaving 19 states that currently sanction the use of corporal punishment in schools.

Despite being on the books in these states, is corporal punishment more policy than practice, existing merely in a school handbook but widely ignored?

Unfortunately, quite the opposite. States that have it, use it, some more than others. During the 2011–2012 school year, 163,000 schoolchildren were subject to corporal punishment.

The widespread use probably comes as a surprise to many people, says Dr. Elizabeth Gershoff, a developmental psychologist at the University of Texas at Austin.

Gershoff, along with Sarah Font, assistant professor of psychology at Pennsylvania State University, recently analyzed data from the U.S. Department of Education Civil Rights Office to pinpoint the prevalence of corporal punishment in schools and presented their findings in a report published by the Society for Research in Child Development.

"Most people assume that corporal punishment has already been abolished across the U.S. Even people in states where it is legal do not always know it is so," explains Gershoff. "We know that it is increasingly being used only in rural areas, which means fewer children and families have experience with it, and that may have contributed to its falling from view."

Corporal punishment is concentrated in southern states and, to a lesser extent, in some states out west. More than half the school districts in Mississippi, Arkansas, and Alabama, use corporal punishment, a level that surprised Gershoff.

"I had assumed it would be only a few pockets of districts still using corporal punishment within each state, but the district-level data we analyzed made clear that the practice is much more widespread in some states than I expected."

Most alarming are the blaring racial disparities in how this punishment is meted out. Students of color, predominantly African American boys, are on the receiving end of a paddle significantly more often than their white counterparts. In Mississippi and Alabama, Black students are 51% more likely to be hit than White students in more than half of those state's districts. In one-fifth of districts, that likelihood soars to 500%.

This is a disparity that cannot be explained away by Black students attending schools more likely to use the punishment—because they don't. Across the South, White students are more likely to attend these schools, according to the report.

Children with disabilities are also at greater risk. These students are more than 50% more likely to be subjected to corporal punishment than their counterparts without disabilities in 67% of districts in Alabama, 44% in Arkansas, 46% in Mississippi, and 36% in Tennessee.

"The extent of the disparities by gender, race, and particularly disability status were quite surprising and very troubling," says Gershoff.

And all for a practice that, according to research, is not only counterproductive from a classroom discipline standpoint, but is

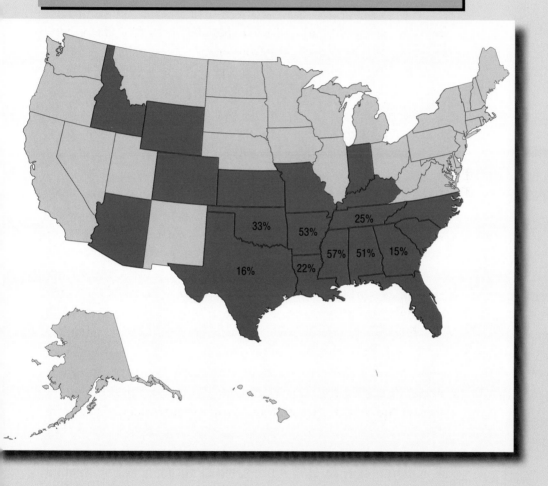

33%

53%

25%

57%   51%   15%

16%

22%

Source: NEA Today

also potentially very damaging—psychologically and physically—to students. (The National Education Association is opposed to corporal punishment, calling it "ineffective" and "harmful.")

Yet, there it is, in 19 states being used fairly regularly in many districts. It's fair to ask: What is going on?

Obviously, administrators permit corporal punishment in schools because they think it is effective. They do this without hard evidence, says Gershoff. "It's just based on gut feeling and their own observations."

For many, the appeal of corporal punishment is that it almost always gets a reaction from children, which sends an immediate signal to parents or educators that they were able to get their point across.

"Unfortunately, what the adult cannot see is that either the child did not internalize how they should behave in the future, or they are resentful of being physically harmed and emotionally shamed, and days or weeks later they repeat or even escalate their misbehavior," adds Gershoff.

Dr. Amir Whitaker, an attorney at the Southern Poverty Law Center who has studied the effects of paddling, recently told Alabama.com, "Research clearly says you're more likely to be aggressive if someone is aggressive with you. You're more likely to physically abuse someone if someone has physically abused you."

Furthermore, corporal punishment often isn't the "last resort" when all other actions to curb serious misbehavior have failed. The available data makes it clear that, yes, students get paddled for offenses such as drunkenness, fighting, and bullying. But many are subject to being hit for minor violations such as cell phone use, inappropriate language, running in hallways, sleeping in class—even failing to turn in homework.

As Gershoff and Font point out, in most states—including those that allow the practice—corporal punishment is banned in many publicly-funded settings that care for children, including child care centers and juvenile detention facilities. (Not to mention the fact that the practice is considered a human rights violation in accordance with the U.S. Treaty on the Rights of the Child.) But this concern does not extend to kids in public schools, at least in more than one-third of the country.

Gershoff believes a national ban on corporal punishment in all schools would be the most comprehensive approach to ending the practice, but because it would have to move through the

U.S. Congress, passing such legislation presents an enormously formidable challenge. Similarly, there have been very few recent attempts in any of the 19 states to institute a ban. Overturn *Ingraham v. Wright* in the Supreme Court? Maybe, but no case dealing with corporal punishment has made it to the Court since that 1977 decision.

Still, all options are possible and realistic, depending on how aware individuals and communities are that corporal punishment is being widely and unfairly used and often at shocking and disturbing levels.

"We have to continue to call attention to this and encourage both state and federal governments to re-examine whether this is how we want to continue treating children in our public schools," says Gershoff.

TEN

Rules Are Changing for Transgender Students

Rebecca Hersher and Carrie Johnson

Recently the rights of LGBTQ students—particularly those of transgender students—have been tested in the US courts. In the following viewpoint, Rebecca Hersher and Carrie Johnson report on the action taken in the early days of the Trump administration to reverse guidance issued by the Obama administration. In 2016, schools were advised that Title IX protects the rights of transgender students to use bathrooms that correspond to their gender identities. As these authors point out, the American Civil Liberties Union expects the Obama administration's interpretation of Title IX to be held up in court. Hersher and Johnson are reporters for National Public Radio (NPR).

The Trump administration is rescinding protections for transgender students in public schools.

The move by the Justice and Education departments reverses guidance the Obama administration publicized in May 2016, which said a federal law known as Title IX protects the right of transgender students to use restrooms and locker rooms that match their gender identities.

But on Wednesday, the two federal departments said the Obama documents do not "contain extensive legal analysis or explain how the position is consistent with the express language

Should transgender students be permitted to use the restrooms they are more comfortable in? Why or why not?

of Title IX, nor did they undergo any formal public process. This interpretation has given rise to significant litigation regarding school restrooms and locker rooms."

A letter issued by the departments also says there "must be due regard for the primary role of states and local school districts in establishing educational policy."

"The president has made it clear throughout the campaign that he's a firm believer in states' rights and that certain issues like this are not best dealt with at the federal level," said White House spokesman Sean Spicer.

About 150,000 young people ages 13 to 17 identify as transgender, according to the Williams Institute at the UCLA School of Law.

Civil rights groups say they worry that the reversal could lead to bullying and violence against vulnerable transgender kids. Some protested outside the White House on Wednesday evening.

When then-President Barack Obama issued the guidelines last year, the White House directed schools to allow students to use the restrooms and locker rooms that match their gender identities, citing a federal law that protects students from gender discrimination.

As NPR's Scott Horsley reported, the Obama administration "warned that schools that defied the recommendation could be at risk of losing federal funds. Thirteen states challenged the Obama guidelines, and a Texas judge put them on hold."

That administration said the directive was meant to help school districts avoid running afoul of civil rights laws, as we reported.

Under Obama, the Department of Justice sued the state of North Carolina over its so-called bathroom law, which prohibits municipal governments in the state from passing laws protecting the rights of transgender people. It also requires trans people in government facilities to use the bathroom corresponding to the sex on their birth certificate.

North Carolina has lost business over the law, including NCAA championship events that were scheduled to be held in the state.

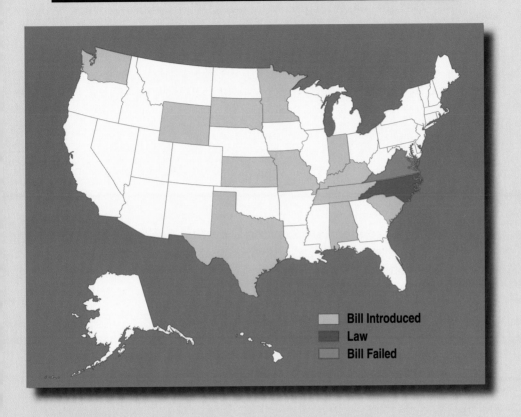

States with antitrans bathroom bills as of February 2017

Bill Introduced
Law
Bill Failed

Source: GLSEN

State legislatures in New Hampshire, Colorado and Texas, among other states, have also considered bills that would restrict access to restrooms for transgender people.

On March 28, the Supreme Court is scheduled to hear oral arguments in a lawsuit filed by a high school student in Virginia. As NPR's Nina Totenberg has reported:

> Gavin Grimm, a 17-year-old senior in Gloucester County, [Va.] ... came out as transgender when he was a freshman

in high school. The school principal allowed him to use the boys' bathroom, until some parents complained, and the school board adopted a policy that required students to use the bathroom that corresponds with their biological sex, or a separate single-stall restroom office.

Grimm sued the school board. His lawsuit argues the bathroom policy is unconstitutional under the 14th Amendment and violates Title IX of the U.S. Education Amendments of 1972, which prohibits sex discrimination by schools.

In April, the 4th U.S. Circuit Court of Appeals allowed the case to proceed. In August, the Supreme Court ruled 5–3 that the school board did not have to allow Grimm to use the restroom of his choice in the interim.

Justice Stephen Breyer said he voted to stay the lower court order as a "courtesy" to maintain the status quo while the court considered whether to hear the lawsuit, as *The Two-Way* reported.

Wednesday's documents say the Trump administration will "more completely consider the legal issues involved" in the Obama rules and in litigation "will not rely on the views expressed within them."

The American Civil Liberties Union's James Esseks says in a statement:

"While it's disappointing to see the Trump administration revoke the guidance, the administration cannot change what Title IX means. When it decided to hear Gavin Grimm's case, the Supreme Court said it would decide which interpretation of Title IX is correct, without taking any administration's guidance into consideration. We're confident that the law is on Gavin's side and he will prevail just as he did in the Fourth Circuit."

ELEVEN

Compassion Is Called for in Dealing with Transgender Students' Bathroom Rights

Judith Valente

> In the following viewpoint, Judith Valente looks at the land-scape of transgender rights in schools around the United States. This piece was written in 2016, not long after the Obama administration issued its guidance to public schools. In her plea to address the matter with understanding and justice, the author directly addresses Catholic educators, uses examples and quotes from transgender students themselves, and advises her readers to come up with a response to the issue that is both fair and compassionate. Valente is a journalist, poet, essayist, retreat leader, and inspirational speaker.

The question of whether transgender individuals can use the bathroom of their choice is shaping up as a battle between states' rights and the federal government. North Carolina is currently suing the federal government, saying it overstepped its authority by trying to prevent the state from requiring transgender individuals to use the bathroom that corresponds with their birth gender.

The federal government says North Carolina's law, and others like it, amount to sex-based discrimination. It has threatened to withhold funds.

"Schools: the next big arena for the transgender debate," by Judith Valente, America Press, Inc., May 13, 2016. Reprinted by permission.

Transgender athletes should be allowed to use locker rooms that align with their gender identities, according to the Obama administration's guidelines.

On May 13 the debate stepped up another notch when in a surprise move the Obama administration issued guidance directing public schools to allow transgender students to use bathrooms and locker rooms consistent with their chosen gender identity. The guidance from leaders at the departments of Education and Justice says public schools are obligated to treat transgender students in a way that matches their gender identity, even if their education records or identity documents indicate a different sex.

According to the administration, the guidelines are meant to ensure that "transgender students enjoy a supportive and nondiscriminatory school environment."

Even before the latest move by the Obama administration, school systems across the country had been re-evaluating their policies regarding bathrooms and locker rooms. Their response could offer clues as to how the question ultimately gets resolved.

Several Midwest schools began examining their policies in the wake of a case in Palatine, Ill., a largely white, affluent community in the northwest suburbs of Chicago. The issue was whether a Palatine High School student transitioning from male to female would be allowed to change in the girls' locker room.

The teen, identified only as "Student A" in public documents, was already playing on a girls' athletic team. She had been on a regimen of female hormones since middle school and has an official diagnosis of gender dysphoria—a severe discomfort with one's birth gender. School records identified her as female.

The civil rights office of the U.S. Education Department found that excluding Student A from the girls' locker room violated Title IX, which prohibits sex-based discrimination in sports. The department threatened to withhold funding. Ultimately, the school district reached a compromise. It agreed to allow the student to change clothes in the locker room, behind a curtain.

Changing hearts has proved another matter. Six female students sent a protest letter to the local school board. "Although we will never fully understand your personal struggle," they said, addressing the transgender student in their letter, "Please understand that we, too, all are experiencing personal struggles that need to be respected."

The girls told the school board, "It is unfair to infringe upon the rights of others to accommodate one person."

School systems across the country have noted the Education Department's threat to Palatine. Some are responding proactively.

Unlike Chicago, central Illinois is a largely socially conservative, Republican-leaning agricultural area of the state. Unit 5, one of the largest school districts in that part of the state, recently

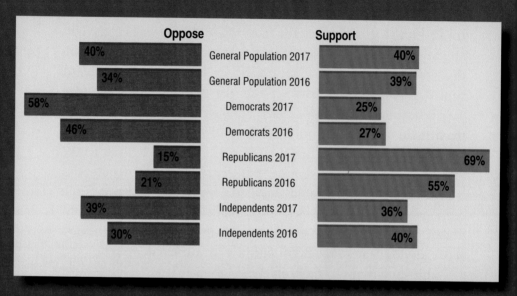

Percentage of Americans who favor and oppose laws that would require transgender people to use the bathroom corresponding with their birth gender

	Oppose		Support
General Population 2017	40%		40%
General Population 2016	34%		39%
Democrats 2017	58%		25%
Democrats 2016	46%		27%
Republicans 2017	15%		69%
Republicans 2016	21%		55%
Independents 2017	39%		36%
Independents 2016	30%		40%

Source: YouGov

amended its bathroom and locker room policies to accommodate transgender students. District 87, a nearby school system, is also considering a change.

"We're trying to create an environment where students can be educated without fear of being harassed and bullied and be free to be who they are," Unit 5's attorney and human resources director Curt Richardson told me.

Unit 5 wasn't under threat of a lawsuit and did not face a noisy public outcry for more liberal bathroom rules. But the Palatine case weighed heavily in its decision, Richardson said. "This is a developing area of the law. So we were trying to be on the forefront of that and be progressive," he said.

Some parents have expressed concern. Richardson says he tells them, "If you've ever been around trans individuals, the amount of harassment they receive is just tremendous and then [there is] the correlation to suicide rates among transgender individuals. So you have to ask yourself, why would anyone subject themselves to that kind of harassment just to get in the girl's restroom?"

It is likely only a matter of time before the debate over transgender rights arises in Catholic schools. It is already happening.

I recently spoke with a student from an Illinois Catholic high school who was born female and now identifies as male. The student said administrators were uncomfortable discussing the transgender experience, let alone changes to bathroom or locker room policies. He said he had been sent home on one occasion for wearing a suit and tie to a school dance. Many teachers and students, he said, continue to call him by his female given name, though he had asked to be called by his preferred male name.

"It's really hard to be in class and just trying to learn, and somebody calls out your birth name and it's like, oh, that's not my name," the student said. "It's really embarrassing and it makes me feel bad. And even though it's all the time, it still hurts."

The student is active in several school clubs and has many friends among classmates but says he is considering transferring to another school for senior year. He wishes he could stay. "This is not something that is new, this is not some phase or fad that is going on right now. These are my feelings, this is who I am, this is part of me and part of the world," the student said. "There are so many people that are like me that are normal, people who just want to live their lives and not be hurt every day."

Unit 5's process could serve as a model for other school systems and private schools. The transgender policy changes were made after a year of extensive consultations between school officials and transgender rights activists, including graduates of Unit 5 schools. The policy only covers students who have an official diagnosis of gender dysphoria or who already have changed their gender on a document such as a birth certificate or driver's license.

Cameron Hurley, a transgender graduate of Unit 5 schools who worked for the changes, said Catholic and private schools don't face the same pressure as publicly funded schools to accommodate transgender students. In the case of Catholic schools, transgender students who seek change will have to "fight on their own. It's going to have to be a private fight outside of government," he said.

Hurley says one of the biggest arguments for giving transgender individuals the right to choose their restroom is that they put themselves at risk if they use a bathroom that corresponds with their anatomy but not how they look.

"I pass as male, and if you're going to force me to use the women's restroom because I haven't changed my anatomy to your liking that could be reported as a man in the women's restroom, and then it becomes dangerous when police become involved in things like that," Hurley said.

"Trans people are like everyone else. They want to go into the bathroom, do what they have to do and get out," Hurley added. In states that have anti-discrimination laws, there have been no reported incidents of anyone being attacked by a transgender person in a public restroom, he said.

Some 200 cities and 17 states have adopted measures allowing transgender people to use the public bathrooms of their choice. And though a backlash has begun—witness the North Carolina law among others—the debate isn't going away. Instead of ignoring the issue, Catholic schools would do well now to begin to formulate a compassionate response.

TWELVE

Students' Right to Read and Teachers' Right to Teach, Not as Straightforward as One Might Think

Kathy Durbin

> In the following viewpoint, Kathy Durbin addresses what is perhaps the strangest right of all to be questioned: the right of students to read. Over the years, people—from both sides of the political spectrum—have demanded that certain books be removed from school bookshelves and not be taught in classrooms. But do students have a right to be exposed to certain works of literature? In this blog post from the web site of Teaching Tolerance, a project of the Southern Poverty Law Center, the author examines the history and potential consequences of challenges to books and the teachers who teach them. Durbin is a journalist and author living in the Pacific Northwest.

Eleanor Cumberland recalls vividly the school desegregation wars that erupted in the farming community of Hillsboro, Ohio, a half-century ago.

In 1954, the year she entered 7th grade, her mother, Imogene Curtis, helped mobilize a campaign of daily marches by black

"Books Under Fire," by Kathy Durbin. Reprinted with permission of Teaching Tolerance, a project of the Southern Poverty Law Center. http://www.tolerance.org/magazine /number-27-spring-2005/feature/books-under-fire.

What rights do students have to read books that their schools have banned or challenged?

students to whites-only schools. Turned away at the schoolhouse door, Curtis and other black parents home-schooled their children and, with help from the NAACP, brought the first civil rights lawsuit in the North under the U.S. Supreme Court's 1954 *Brown v. Board of Education* ruling. Eleanor Cumberland's house was used as a makeshift school during the protracted legal battle.

So it was with full awareness of the history of the civil rights struggle that the 63-year-old retired nurse's aide in 2004 asked Hillsboro High Principal Larry Stall to remove Harper Lee's *To Kill a Mockingbird* from the 9th-grade English curriculum.

The critically acclaimed novel, set in the fictional Alabama community of Maycomb during the Great Depression, tells the story of a town torn by the trial of a black man wrongly accused of raping a white woman; of Atticus Finch, the white lawyer who defends him; and of his children, Jem and Scout, through whose voices the events unfold.

To Kill a Mockingbird consistently ranks near the top of the American Library Association's list of 100 most frequently banned books. Most complaints involve the use of language now considered racially offensive, including the N-word.

"I feel the book serves no purpose but to keep racism and separatism alive in a day when we're supposed to be teaching love and equality," Cumberland said in a letter to the principal. "In all reality, we know these feelings of hatred and prejudice are still harbored by some people, but should those responsible for our children's education play a part in keeping bigotry, superiority and hatred alive?"

"*To Kill a Mockingbird* is a work of art that clearly confronts racism," Superintendent Byron Wisecup responded. "The highest result of education is teaching tolerance. This book is unflinching in its condemnation of racial prejudice."

At the recommendation of a review committee, he kept the book in the curriculum.

To Kill a Mockingbird is in good company. Mark Twain's *Adventures of Huckleberry Finn*, J.D. Salinger's *The Catcher in the Rye* and J. K. Rowling's wildly popular *Harry Potter* series routinely make the ALA's list of most-challenged books.

Rooted in History

Notwithstanding the First Amendment, book banning is a practice rooted in American history. In 1873, Congress passed the Comstock Law in an effort to legislate public morality. Though rarely enforced, the act remains on the books.

A survey by the National School Boards Association found that one-third of challenges to school reading materials in the 1990s resulted in the withdrawal or restriction of those materials.

The reasons people try to censor or restrict access haven't changed all that much over time. Books are most often attacked for being "age-inappropriate" in their use of sexually explicit or racially charged language or for expressing unorthodox political, religious or cultural views. Some challenges are brought by individual parents, others by religious right groups that target books they regard as anti-Christian.

Whatever the motive, efforts to restrict access to books deemed objectionable can polarize communities, leaving deep wounds. Classroom teachers often find themselves on the front line in these battles, yet without any real power to defend their choices or to affect the outcome—an uncomfortable place to be.

Teachers no longer get fired for teaching Aldous Huxley's *Brave New World,* but most teacher contracts still don't adequately protect academic freedom, said Ann Nice, president of the Portland, Ore., Association of Teachers. Her union's contract allows members to introduce controversial materials provided they "are appropriate and relevant to course content and grade level and that balanced viewpoints on a controversial issue are presented."

That language did not prevent a months-long public debate in Portland in the fall of 2002, after a parent and two African American students challenged the way *Adventures of Huckleberry Finn* was being taught in a 9th-grade class at predominantly white Lincoln High School. Mark Twain's classic tale of a runaway slave uses the N-word more than 200 times.

The book was not removed, but student activists gathered 260 signatures on a petition to the school board asking that teachers

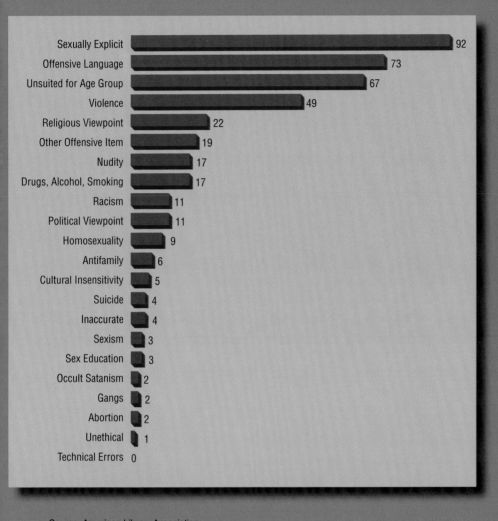

Common reasons for challenging books

Sexually Explicit	92
Offensive Language	73
Unsuited for Age Group	67
Violence	49
Religious Viewpoint	22
Other Offensive Item	19
Nudity	17
Drugs, Alcohol, Smoking	17
Racism	11
Political Viewpoint	11
Homosexuality	9
Antifamily	6
Cultural Insensitivity	5
Suicide	4
Inaccurate	4
Sexism	3
Sex Education	3
Occult Satanism	2
Gangs	2
Abortion	2
Unethical	1
Technical Errors	0

Source: American Library Association

who use it undergo sensitivity training. Even state legislators joined the debate.

Tracey Wyatt, an 18-year classroom veteran, was one of four Lincoln High English teachers who publicly supported the embattled teacher. "It could have happened to any one of us," she said.

None of the teachers stopped using *Adventures of Huckleberry Finn* as a result of the controversy, she said; in fact, her own students expressed a strong desire to read it. Lincoln teachers prepared their students by discussing Twain's use of language and describing race relations in the post-Civil War era—just as they did before the challenge flared into the headlines, Wyatt said.

High school students are ready to handle sexual, racial and other sensitive content, she said. "I don't want to bombard them. But I don't feel I need to protect them as long as I have built this safe place for them to discuss these issues. That's the key."

Wyatt added, "Some people say, 'Have them read it in college.' I don't think postponing important discussions until college is the right thing to do."

In Federal Way, Wash., 9th-grade English teacher Vince Halloran found himself in the spotlight in the spring of 2004 after 32 parents upset about sexual content in the book *Balzac and the Little Chinese Seamstress* petitioned the superintendent to remove it from the reading list. The novel by Dai Sijie, which tells the story of two youths who find a suitcase full of banned books during China's Cultural Revolution, came highly recommended by the school district's head of curriculum and instruction. After the complaint was filed, a committee that reevaluated the book gave it unanimous support.

Nonetheless, the superintendent not only agreed to remove the book but directed that, in the future, the district would provide reading lists to parents in advance and submit them to the school board for approval.

Halloran said the decision to appease the complaining parents deeply disappointed him. It also had a chilling effect, he said, "not just because teachers and students lost a precious and powerful resource, but because it seemed very clear that what mattered during this episode was who could raise the biggest stink. Reason and logic seemed to be thrown out the window."

Acting Unilaterally

Most school districts have established processes for handling complaints about course materials. If a parent objects, a teacher may assign an alternative reading. The next step typically is a formal review by a committee of principals and curriculum specialists. Finally, a parent may appeal to an elected school board and make the case for the book's removal at a public hearing where all sides get to have their say.

Complaints most often escalate into controversy when an individual teacher, principal, superintendent or school board member, responding to political pressure, bypasses that process and acts unilaterally.

That's what happened in the Savannah-Chatham County, Ga., Public Schools in 1999 after a stepfather offended by what he regarded as profanity, explicit sex and extreme violence in three books on his stepdaughter's advanced-placement reading list bypassed the teacher, principal and superintendent and went straight to the school board. At a televised meeting, he read selected passages aloud, embarrassing board members. Soon after, the principal was ordered to pull the books. Eventually, the decision was rescinded.

"The Schoolhouse Gate"

In 1982, the U.S. Supreme Court sent a mixed message on the issue in a New York case challenging a decision by the Island Trees Union Free School District Board of Education to order nine books removed from junior high and high school libraries.

The high court agreed that school boards have considerable discretion to determine school curricula and to decide what books are available in school libraries based on "community values." However, a majority found that it was a violation of the First Amendment for a school board to deny students access to ideas by ordering books removed from library shelves simply because board members disagreed with those ideas.

Citing a previous court ruling, Justice William Brennan wrote that students do not "shed their constitutional rights to freedom of speech or expression at the schoolhouse gate." However, the court did not address challenges to books assigned by classroom teachers.

And students are not oblivious to the message sent when a book is removed from the classroom, English teacher Halloran said.

"Students already intuit that what they are getting is divorced from and bears scant resemblance to the 'real world,'" he said. "Why not stand firm as a public institution that expresses and explores the complex range of human experience? Why be diplomatic and apologetic about the fact that we do not shy away from difficult, challenging and complex topics?"

The American Library Association's list of the 100 most challenged books is drawn from more than 6,000 challenges reported from 1990–2000 by the ALA's Office for Intellectual Freedom. Research suggests for each challenge reported, there are as many as four or five unreported.

What You Should Know about Student Rights

Facts about the First Amendment

- Freedom of religion is the first freedom mentioned in the First Amendment to the US Constitution.

- In addition to freedom of religion and speech, the First Amendment also guarantees freedom of the press, the right to assemble peacefully, and the right to petition the government if you believe your rights have been violated.

- Freedom of speech is understood to mean expression of any kind, not just verbal speech. Writing, and wearing slogans or symbols on clothes have been protected under the constitutional protection of freedom of speech.

- The First Amendment also protects your right *not to speak*—for example by not saying the Pledge of Allegiance or saluting the flag.

- Expressing protest by burning the flag is protected by the First Amendment.

- Obscene speech is not protected by the First Amendment, nor is speech that is intended to incite violence.

- Private schools are not under the same restrictions when it comes to freedom of religion as public schools are.

- The First Amendment right to freedom of religion also protects your right to have no religion.

- Public schools can teach *about* religion (its history, literature, and influences) but cannot in any way promote religion.

- The Constitutional provision of freedom of religion was originally intended to protect religions from government interference.

- Scripture readings, prayers, and devotionals (even when nondenominational) are not allowed in public schools.

- Religious clubs are allowed in schools as long as the group's activities are conducted during nonschool hours, school officials are not involved in the club, and the school's facilities are made equally available to all religious groups.

- The US Supreme Court case *Tinker v. Des Moines Independent Community School District* involved Iowa students who protested the Vietnam war by wearing black armbands to school. The court ruled in favor of the students, writing, "It can hardly be argued that either students or teachers shed their constitutional rights to freedom of speech or expression at the schoolhouse gate."

Facts about the Fourth Amendment

- The Fourth Amendment guarantees "the right of the people to be secure in their persons, houses, papers, and effects, against unreasonable searches and seizures."

- The US Supreme Court has ruled that the Fourth Amendment applies to students in public schools in *New Jersey v. T.L.O.* in 1985.

- Since safety in schools is of primary concern, searches may be conducted if reasonable suspicion is present and justified.

- The use of drug-sniffing dogs in public schools is allowable.

- Students have the right to remain silent when interrogated by officials.

- Blanket searches can be conducted also as a preventative measure. This would include metal detectors and bag checks at school entrances.

- The US Supreme Court case *Verona School District 47J v. Acton* upheld the constitutionality of random drug testing among student athletes in an Oregon public school. The court ruled that although drug testing is a form of search, the search was reasonable.

Facts about Title IX

- Title IX is a federal statute that prohibits discrimination on the basis of sex in any federally funded educational program.
- While Title IX is best known for prohibiting sex discrimination in sports, it prohibits sex discrimination in all aspects of education.
- The Obama administration used Title IX in its guidelines for how schools should handle bathroom facilities for transgender students.

Facts about Freedom of Speech Online

- Freedom of speech online is somewhat new territory, and so far rulings have been somewhat contradictory.

Facts about Student Journalism

- Student journalists are responsible for taking steps to avoid libel and defamation just as professional journalists are.
- All fifty states, the District of Columbia, and the federal government, have open meeting laws (often called "sunshine laws") that require meetings of government officials be open to the public and press. Student journalists can use these laws to attend meetings of school boards and other school officials.
- Research has shown that students who work on high school newspapers and yearbooks get better grades, score

higher on college entrance exams, and get better grades when they become college freshmen.

- Underground and independent student publications are also protected from censorship.

Facts about Corporal Punishment in Schools

- Students of color and students with disabilities are disproportionately subjected to corporal punishment in schools.
- There is a significant body of data showing that violent discipline methods are damaging to academic achievement and long-term well-being and are not conducive to a productive learning environment.
- Southern states and some western states are more likely than other regions of the country to have school districts that allow corporal punishment.
- Though students of color are more likely to be victims of corporal punishment than white students, schools that allow corporal punishment are more likely to be in predominately white school districts.

Facts about Banned Books

- Each year the American Library Association sponsors Banned Book Week, a celebration of the right to read.
- The most common reason for banning books is that they are deemed to be "sexually explicit" or contain offensive language.
- *To Kill a Mockingbird* by Harper Lee has been one of the most challenged books for seven decades—as long as it has been in print.
- The Harry Potter series tops the list of most banned books of the twenty-first century.
- In some districts, teachers have been fired for teaching banned books.

- The first recorded book burning in what is now the United States happened in 1650.

Facts about Transgender Rights

- As of March 2017, nineteen states, the District of Columbia, and more than two hundred municipalities have laws that allow transgender people to use facilities that match their preferred gender.

- There is no evidence that transgender protections (which have existed for years) increase the likelihood of assaults.

- Research has shown that not allowing transgender children to live their identity can be harmful, even deadly to those children.

- The National Collegiate Athletic Association (NCAA) allows transgender individuals to participate in sports that accord with their gender identity as long as the individuals are taking hormone therapy.

- According to GLSEN's National School Climate Survey, 35 percent of LGBT students avoid school bathrooms because they feel unsafe or uncomfortable.

What You Should Do About Student Rights

As you can see from the viewpoints you have read, the fact that a right is enshrined in the US Constitution or the Canadian Charter of Rights and Freedoms is no guarantee that it will be respected. Interpreting those rights can sometimes be a challenge, and even when the law is perfectly clear, the debate is not always over. As you can see, the way Americans have viewed freedom of speech and religion (and how carefully the courts have protected it) has varied over the years. The same is true with other rights. Throughout history, the rights of citizens (particularly the right to free expression) have waxed and waned, more likely to be curtailed during times of war and expanded during times of peace. Yet times of war can also be when those rights are tested and come out the stronger for it. *Tinker v. Des Moines*, the landmark case that established free speech rights for students, involved young people wearing black armbands to express their opposition to the Vietnam War.

The discussions and debates our Founding Fathers had over 250 years ago still inform our discussions and debates today, as have 250 years of laws and challenges to those laws that have continued to shape our government. While it might seem comforting to live in a world of concrete answers and clear do's and don'ts, such a world would not, in the long run, be a very nice place to live. Times change, people change, and leaders change. The framers of the Constitution designed that document—and even its Bill of Rights—to be flexible enough to accommodate these changes. Part of being an engaged citizen is knowing and understanding how your government works and what its commitments and traditions are, and that is a more challenging task than many citizens assume. Fortunately, it is also a fascinating and gratifying endeavor.

New technologies and changes in society pose interesting and sometimes vexing challenges for interpreting and protecting basic rights. The internet, social media, and smartphones have added new wrinkles to questions of freedom of speech and the press. A rapidly changing population has required us to take a closer look at what freedom of religion means, and to be ever more vigilant in protecting it. The rights of gay and transgender people are being challenged and affirmed and challenged again. The current debate surrounding hate speech and campus speech codes calls on us to carefully consider the balance of protecting freedom of speech while still protecting our fellow citizens from hate and intolerance. No one said that protecting our rights would ever be easy.

The Founding Fathers could never have imagined digital technology and doubtless would have been surprised (we hope pleasantly) to learn that the rights they spelled out in the Constitution with only white landowners in mind would one day apply to women and the descendants of slaves. And who can imagine what they would have made of the demand for equal rights for transgender people? But even though they couldn't see into the future, they left us room to work with all those changes.

When it comes to interpreting the law and protecting one's rights, very often the matter comes down not just to the letter of the law, but the spirit and legal history behind it. This is why simply having a general and fuzzy notion that you have "freedom of speech" or that "it's a free country" is not enough to give you the tools to protect your rights and those of others. If the protection of individual liberties is important to you, then it is essential that you learn about those rights and how they have been challenged and defended over the years. And like the task of learning how government works, learning how laws have been made, interpreted, and in many cases overturned is fascinating, too. Of course, just knowing how this all works is not enough. You have to be vigilant. That takes being both informed and engaged. If you are concerned about the rights of LGBTQ people, then you need to closely follow cases in which those rights are challenged and speak out about what matters to you. If you are concerned about the large numbers of black youth who are being incarcerated, you need to learn about the background and cases and get involved. If you feel that your right to follow your faith is in danger, you should learn all you can about that issue. If you believe that campus speech codes are eroding free speech or that hate speech is pushing the right to free speech too far, then educate yourself on the issues, and join the conversation. Even if none of the issues that dominate today's headlines grab your attention or call to your heart, if you value any of your own rights or even the concept of having individual rights, you must learn how to protect them as well as the rights of others. Carl Schurz, a nineteenth-century US senator and statesman put it like this, "You cannot subvert your neighbor's rights without striking a dangerous blow at your own." And you cannot protect your own rights while ignoring those of others.

ORGANIZATIONS TO CONTACT

The editors have compiled the following list of organizations concerned with the issues debated in this book. The descriptions are derived from materials provided by the organizations. All have publications or information available for interested readers. The list was compiled on the date of publication of the present volume; the information provided here may change. Be aware that many organizations take several weeks or longer to respond to inquiries, so allow as much time as possible.

Anti-Defamation League
605 3rd Avenue
New York, NY 10158
(212) 885-7700
website: www.adl.org

The Anti-Defamation League (ADL) fights anti-Semitism and all forms of hate. The ADL works with schools to promote respectful, inclusive, and civil environments both inside and outside the classroom.

American Civil Liberties Union
125 Broad Street, 18th Floor
New York, NY 10001
(212) 549-2500
website: www.aclu.org

The American Civil Liberties Union (ACLU) is an organization that works to defend and protect the individual rights and liberties that are guaranteed by the Constitution of the United States. The ACLU publishes a *Students' Rights Handbook* that serves as a valuable resource for students. This booklet discusses student rights, when they can be exercised, and when school officials can limit them, and offers practical tips for students.

American Library Association
50 East Huron Street
Chicago, IL 60611
(800) 545-2433
email: ala@ala.org
website: www.ala.org

The American Library Association (ALA) is a nonprofit association of libraries dedicated to providing leadership and promotion of libraries and information services. The ALA sponsors Banned Books Week, an annual event celebrating the freedom to read.

Canadian Civil Liberties Association
90 Eglinton Ave E.
Toronto, ON M4P 2Y3
Canada
(416) 363-0321
email: mail@ccla.org
website: www.ccla.org

The Canadian Civil Liberties Association is an organization dedicated to fighting for the civil liberties, human rights, and democratic freedoms of people, including students of all ages and levels, all across Canada.

Equality Federation Institute
818 SW 3rd Ave. #141
Portland, Oregon, 97204
(929) 373-3370
email: Mark@equalityfederation.org
website: www.equalityfederation.org

The Equality Federation Institute is an organization dedicated to equal opportunities for LGBTQ people and their families. This includes the rights of students, such as promoting the embrace of transgender students in public schools.

Foundation for Individual Rights in Education (FIRE)
510 Walnut Street
Suite 1250
Philadelphia, PA 19106
(215) 717-3473
email: Fire@thefire.org
website: www.thefire.org

FIRE is a nonprofit dedicated to defending and sustaining individual rights at America's colleges and universities. These rights include freedom of speech, legal equality, due process, religious liberty, and sanctity of conscience—the essential qualities of individual liberty and dignity.

Freechild Project
PO Box 6185
Olympia, WA 98507-6185
(360) 489-9680
email: info@freechild.org
website: www.freechild.org

The Freechild Project advocates for youth and adults to work together to change our world. The organization emphasizes student rights in the enactment of social change.

Leadership Conference on Civil and Human Rights
1620 L Street NW Suite 11000
Washington, DC 20036
(202) 466-3434
website: www.civilrights.org

The Leadership Conference on Civil and Human Rights is a coalition of more than two hundred organizations working to promote and protect the civil and human rights of all people in the United States.

Student Press Law Center
1608 Rhode Island NW, Suite 211
Washington, D. C. 20036
(202) 785-5450
email: splc@splc.org
website: www.splc.org

The Student Press Law Center is a legal assistance agency devoted to educating high school and college journalists about the rights and responsibilities embodied in the First Amendment.

Teaching Tolerance
400 Washington Avenue
Montgomery, Alabama 36104
(888) 414-7752
website: www.splcenter.org/teaching-tolerance

A project of the Southern Poverty Law Center, Teaching Tolerance is a group dedicated to combating prejudice among youth and promoting equality, inclusiveness, and equitable learning environments in the classroom.

United States Student Association
PO Box 33486
Washington, DC 20036
email: ops@usstudents.org
website: www.usstudents.org

The United States Student Association, the country's oldest, largest, and most inclusive national student-led organization, develops current and future leaders and amplifies the student voice at the local, state, and national levels by mobilizing grassroots power to win concrete victories on student issues.

BIBLIOGRAPHY

Books

Floyd Abrams. *The Soul of the First Amendment*. New Haven, CT: Yale University Press, 2017.
Abrams takes a detailed look at the history of free speech and makes a powerful case for the importance of freedom of speech in protecting citizens from the overreach of government. The book addresses current issues such as Wikileaks and Edward Snowden's revelations.

Erwin Chemerinksy and Howard Gillman. *Free Speech on Campus*. New Haven, CT: Yale University Press, 2017.
A timely discussion of issues related to campus free speech, with an emphasis on the balance between supporting the right of freedom of speech and ensuring a safe and inclusive learning environment.

Homer L. Hall, Aaron Manfull, and Megan Fromm. *Student Journalism & Media Literacy*. New York, NY: The Rosen Publishing Group, 2016.
This comprehensive resource covers everything student journalists need to know in a rapidly changing media landscape. Addresses topics that journalists are only now facing such as the rights and responsibilities of citizen journalists, managing a news website, and digital security.

Alexander Hamilton, James Madison, and John Jay. *The Federalist Papers*. (Dover Thrift Edition.) Mineral, NY: Dover Books, 2014.
A collection of essays written anonymously by three of the Founding Fathers about the principles that make up the foundation of the government of the United States. A must for anyone interested in their rights.

John W. Johnson. *The Struggle for Student Rights: Tinker v. Des Moines and the 1960s*. Lawrence, KS: University Press of Kansas, 1997.
In addition to being a thorough and very readable history of the US Supreme Court case of *Tinker v. Des Moines*, this interesting resource brings the period to life with newspaper clippings, interviews, and other important primary sources related to the case.

Anthony Lewis. *Freedom for the Thought We Hate: A Biography of the First Amendment*. New York, NY: Basic, 2010.
An already classic look at the First Amendment by one of its most respected defenders. Lewis argues passionately and eloquently for First Amendment protections, but also points out where he believes limitations to those freedoms are warranted.

Martha M. McCarthy, et al. (Seventh Edition). *Public School Law: Teachers' and Students' Rights*. New York, NY: Pearson, 2013.
The seventh edition of this classic and comprehensive guide to the laws applicable to public school teachers and students.

Daxton R. Stewart. *Social Media and the Law: A Guide for Communication Students and Professionals* (Second Edition). New York, NY: Routledge, 2017.
The second edition of this guide to social media for communications students covers the swiftly changing landscape of legal rights and responsibilities of communications in the digital age.

Bryan R. Warnick. *Understanding Student Rights in Schools: Speech, Religion, and Privacy in Educational Settings*. New York, NY: Teachers College Press, 2013.
A guide for student teachers, but with an excellent discussion of the rights students have and how they can best be protected.

Periodicals and Internet Sources

Melinda D. Anderson, "The Misplaced Fear of Religion in Classrooms." *The Atlantic*, October 19, 2015. https://www.theatlantic.com/education/archive/2015/10/the-misplaced-fear-of-religion-in-classrooms/411094

Evie Blad, "Can schools punish students for protesting the national anthem?" PBS NewsHour, October 7, 2016. http://www.pbs.org/newshour/updates/schools-students-protesting-national-anthem

Nina Burleigh, "The Battle Against 'Hate Speech' on College Campuses Gives Rise to a Generation that Hates Speech." *Newsweek*, May 26, 2016. http://www.newsweek.com/2016/06/03/college-campus-free-speech-thought-police-463536.html

Lauren Camera, "Supreme Court Expands Rights for Students with Disabilities," March 22, 2017. https://www.usnews.com /news/education-news/articles/2017-03-22 /supreme-court-expands-rights-for-students-with-disabilities

Christopher Ingraham, "A Georgia sheriff ordered pat-down searches for every student at a public high school. Now they're suing." *Washington Post*, June 7, 2017. https://www .washingtonpost.com/news/wonk/wp/2017/06/07/a-georgia -sheriff-ordered-hands-on-body-searches-for-every-student -at-a-public-high-school-now -theyre-suing/?utm_term=.71770d9497fe

Stanley Kurtz, "Understanding the Campus Free-Speech Crisis." *National Review*, April 12, 2017. http://www.nationalreview .com/corner/446634/campus-free-speech-crisis

Carolyn Schurr Levin, "Legal analysis: How far can schools go in limiting student speech online?" Southern Poverty Law Center, June 6, 2016. http://www.splc.org/article/2016/06 /legal-analysis-student-speech

Susan Miller, "Beyond the Bathroom: Report Shows Laws' Harm for Transgender Students." *USA Today*, April 11, 2017. https://www.usatoday.com/story/news/nation/2017/04/11 /beyond-bathroom-report-shows-laws-harm-transgender -students/100265266/

New York Times. "Understanding Transgender Access Laws." nytimes.com. February 24, 2017. https://www.nytimes .com/2017/02/24/us/transgender-bathroom-law .html?mcubz=0

Stacey Patton, "Stop Beating Black Children." *New York Times*, March 10, 2017. https://www.nytimes.com/2017/03/10 /opinion/sunday/stop-beating-black-children.html?mcubz=0

Eric Posner, "Universities Are Right—and within Their Rights— To Crack Down on Speech and Behavior." Slate, February 12, 2015. http://www.slate.com/articles/news_and_politics /view_from_chicago/2015/02/university_speech_codes _students_are_children_who_must_be_protected.html

Daniella Silva, "Kansas Principal Resigns after Student Journalists Question Credentials." nbcnews.com, April 5, 2017. http://www.nbcnews.com/news/us-news/kansas -principal-resigns-after-student-journalists-question-creden-tials-n743021

Mark Joseph Stern, "Judges Have No Idea What to Do About Student Speech on the Internet" Slate, February 18, 2016. http://www.slate.com/articles/technology/future _tense/2016/02/in_bell_v_itawamba_county_school_board_ scotus_may_rule_on_the_first_amendment.html

Cory Turner, "These States Allow Teachers and Staff to Hit Students." NPR, December 1, 2016. http:// www.npr.org/sections/ed/2016/12/01/503749071/ these-states-allow-schools-to-hit-students

Maryellen Weimer, "Student Rights and the Role of Faculty," Faculty Focus, May 10, 2017. https://www.facultyfocus.com /articles/teaching-professor-blog/student-rights-role-faculty

Linda K. Wertheimer, "Schools Shouldn't Preach. But They Should Teach Kids about Religion." *Washington Post*, September 8, 2015. https://www.washingtonpost.com /posteverything/wp/2015/09/08/schools-shouldnt -preach-but-they-should-teach-about-religion/?utm _term=.7623728ee603

David R. Wheeler, "Do Students Still Have Free Speech in School?" *The Atlantic*, April 7, 2014. https://www.theatlantic .com/education/archive/2014/04/do-students-still-have-free-speech-in-school/360266/

Websites

Combating Discrimination and Protecting Religious Freedom. The US Department of Justice.
(https://www.justice.gov/crt/combating-religious-discrimination-and-protecting-religious-freedom-20)
The US Department of Justice explains the laws that protect religious freedom in schools and how the government goes about enforcing those laws and protecting the rights of citizens. Specific

cases are detailed here, and many links to further information are provided. This site offer an interesting insight into the workings of the Justice Department as it relates to protecting educational rights.

The Constitution of the United States (National Archives)
(https://www.archives.gov/founding-docs/constitution-transcript)
In addition to a transcription of the original text of the US Constitution (with the original spelling), this site of the government archives contains links to additional founding documents. Readers will also enjoy the high-resolution images of the original documents and interesting articles on the framers.

The First Amendment in Schools: A Resource Guide. National Coalition Against Censorship.
(http://ncac.org/resource/first-amendment-in-schools)
This guide to censorship in schools contains many links with a wealth of information, including history, data, policies, and case studies. Readers will learn not only how the First Amendment came to be, but how it has been interpreted and applied over the years.

Thomas Jefferson: Establishing a Federal Republic: Library of Congress
(https://www.loc.gov/exhibits/jefferson/jefffed.html)
This collection of primary documents related to Thomas Jefferson's contributions to the establishment of the US Constitution provides fascinating insight into the debate among the Founding Fathers about the shape of the government of the United States. Many familiar quotes from Thomas Jefferson are brought to life by the images of the original documents.

Vietnam War, student protests of, 11, 37, 90, 94

W

Westside Community Board of Education v. Mergens, 15–16
West Virginia v. Barnette, 21, 22

Z

zero-tolerance policies, 11